Solving the
People Puzzle

Solving the People Puzzle

Cultural Intelligence and Special Operations Forces

Dr. Emily Spencer

DUNDURN PRESS
TORONTO

Copy Editor: Cheryl Hawley
Design: Jennifer Scott
Printer: Marquis

Library and Archives Canada Cataloguing in Publication

Spencer, Emily
    Solving the people puzzle : cultural intelligence and special operations forces / Emily Spencer.

Includes bibliographical references and index.
ISBN 978-1-55488-750-7

    1. Cultural awareness. 2. Cultural competence. 3. Intercultural communication. 4. Special forces (Military science). I. Title.

U163.S64 2010   355.3'43   C2009-907471-0

1   2   3   4   5   14   13   12   11   10

We acknowledge the support of the **Canada Council for the Arts** and the **Ontario Arts Council** for our publishing program. We also acknowledge the financial support of the **Government of Canada** through the **Canada Book Fund** and **The Association for the Export of Canadian Books**, and the **Government of Ontario** through the **Ontario Book Publishers Tax Credit** program, and the **Ontario Media Development Corporation**.

Printed and bound in Canada.
www.dundurn.com

Dundurn Press	Gazelle Book Services Limited	Dundurn Press
3 Church Street, Suite 500	White Cross Mills	2250 Military Road
Toronto, Ontario, Canada	High Town, Lancaster, England	Tonawanda, NY
M5E 1M2	LA1 4XS	U.S.A. 14150

Contents

Foreword

I am delighted to introduce *Solving the People Puzzle*. By examining the topic of cultural intelligence (CQ) from the standpoint of special operations forces (SOF), this book goes to the heart of operations in the contemporary security environment in several important ways. First, it focuses on the human element, which is, after all, the core strength of SOF the world over. Second, it speaks directly to the primary, and pivotal, component of the SOF mantra of think, move, communicate, shoot. Finally, this volume captures the SOF emphasis on fundamental conceptual philosophies such as the indirect approach and integrated operations.

The application of CQ defined as "the ability to recognize the shared beliefs, values, attitudes, and behaviours of a group of people and, most importantly, to apply that knowledge toward a specific goal," should prove to be a most welcome formalization and addition to the SOF skill set. After all, SOF is a strategic asset, and its operations are both intelligence-driven and human-centric. As such, it is absolutely vital that SOF operators, enablers, and leadership fully utilize CQ to maximize operational effectiveness and mission success.

It has long been acknowledged that the greatest strength that SOF possesses is not its technologically advanced equipment, platforms, or weaponry, but rather its personnel. In this vein, CQ provides another tool to build the cognitive strength and effectiveness of our SOF men and women in the current ambiguous, uncertain, volatile, and ever-changing security environment. It represents a force multiplier that will assist in potentially alleviating the need for kinetic solutions; however, should that not be possible, it also enables SOF to ensure that its actions are as surgically precise as possible. In the end, it is an important enabler in ensuring that SOF consistently "do more good than harm" to achieve its nation's aims.

Solving the People Puzzle is an important addition to the scholarly body of knowledge on military affairs. Such knowledge and understanding are essential for the proper conduct of national security affairs, and education is the key to success in today's challenging environment. This means, as the book also rightly stresses, a reliance on "more than just equipping and training soldiers to fight with the most advanced technology and weapons systems available. It requires military personnel who are well trained and equipped, but also well educated. It demands individuals who are not only capable, but who thrive in ambiguity, complexity, and change."

I therefore recommend this book to all military personnel, whether SOF or conventional, as well as those who interact with, or are interested in, the profession of arms. It provides insight and an important philosophical, if not doctrinal, foundation to CQ that must be embraced by SOF, as well as by all military professionals, to ensure that we provide our men and women, and the nation itself, with the greatest chance of success in operations in a very challenging security environment now and into the future.

Joel Sokolsky, Ph.D
Principal
Royal Military College of Canada

Acknowledgements

First, I wish to thank the men and women of the Canadian Forces. Without the courage, tenacity, and sacrifice of these individuals there would be no need for this type of scholarship. Their efforts on behalf of all Canadians are truly noteworthy.

In particular, however, I would like to take this opportunity to sincerely thank Colonel Bernd Horn, the former deputy commander, Canadian Special Operations Forces Command (CANSOFCOM), for his generous feedback and guidance throughout the writing process. This book would not have been possible without his support and encouragement. I know that I am a better person for this experience — thank you!

Finally, I wish to thank the design and editing team, specifically Cheryl Hawley at Dundurn Press, for turning the raw manuscript into the polished volume you have before you.

Introduction

Militaries spend enormous amounts of money, time, and energy ensuring that their troops are trained on weapon systems, vehicles, and equipment. They spend small fortunes on preparatory exercises and training to test tactics, techniques, and procedures (TTPs); drills; and general soldier proficiency and effectiveness should they need to exercise force protection, demonstrate a deterrent posture, or actually fight during an operation. This preparation and expenditure is only prudent. It makes perfect sense, particularly when lives are at risk. It is, after all, just due diligence. Moreover, it better positions an organization to be successful on operations. However, what makes less sense is that, comparatively speaking, very little effort, if any, is spent solving the "people puzzle."

In reality, most stability and counter-insurgency operations are all about the people. People are one, if not *the*, key component to mission success in the contemporary operating environment (COE), a space characterized by complexity, ambiguity, volatility, change, and danger. People are important at all levels, whether dealing with adversaries, the host nation population, the international community, or even one's own nation. To be successful in these potentially diverse environments, cultural intelligence (CQ) — that is, the ability to recognize the shared beliefs, values, attitudes, and behaviours of a group of people and, most importantly, to apply that knowledge toward a specific goal — is critical.

The fact is, understanding the people you work with — whether other Canadians, international alliance members, or host nation inhabitants — makes for smoother relationships, better communication and comprehension, and, therefore, more effective results. Grasping differences in how others think, behave, make decisions, view the world, and interpret actions assists in providing strategies and options for how best to engage them to achieve your own objectives. Effective relationships, based on high levels of CQ, will assist in gaining support for operations, whether in the form of co-operation, information, or participation. Enhanced CQ will also enhance communications and interaction and have a direct impact on improved human relations. High levels of CQ will ensure that both parties actually communicate and hear what is meant rather than simply what is being said. In essence, CQ helps to mitigate the gulf between the "intended message" and the "received message." Proper interpersonal skills (i.e., informal personal chat prior to getting to business), verbal expressions understood by both parties (i.e., avoiding jargon or slang known only to one party and that may have ambiguous or potentially negative meaning to another), and proper body language (i.e., that may be innocuous to one party but offensive to another or, conversely, understanding and accepting practices in other cultures that are alien to your own) will enhance clarity and effectiveness of communication and ensure there is less confusion or breakdown due simply to misunderstanding.

Furthermore, a better understanding of one's adversaries is equally as empowering. Abandoning preconceived, superficial, or erroneous perceptions and making an effort to fully comprehend the "enemy" can provide invaluable insights into their attitudes, behaviours, decision making, and motivations. This knowledge can provide options and strategies for disrupting, neutralizing, and defeating adversaries by addressing real or perceived grievances, discrediting their informational/ideological messages with erosion of support bases, disrupting their decision-making processes and alliances, and possibly co-opting the more moderate adversarial membership.

There is no group in the military for which these connections are more important than special operations forces (SOF). SOF are comprised of highly trained personnel with an ability to deploy rapidly and apply special skills sets in a variety of environments and circumstances to achieve surgical precision non-kinetic and kinetic effects in peace, conflict, or war. Moreover, despite the focus on technologically advanced equipment, SOF's philosophical and practical adherence to its core strength — namely its emphasis on cognitive responses to ambiguous and complex situations and its reliance on individuals who are adaptive, innovative, and agile — make it the ideal counter to an uncertain present and future battle space that is won or lost in the human dimension. In fact, one of the principle SOF "truths" is that humans are more important than hardware. SOF equips and enables the man; it does not man the equipment.

Therefore, it is not difficult to understand the natural relationship between CQ and SOF. After all, the COE is inextricably fuelled by human problems and, therefore, needs a human solution. As such, it seems completely logical to empower SOF, the "force of choice," with CQ, the "tool of choice." Solving the people puzzle — that is, using an understanding of the beliefs, values, attitudes, and behaviours of others to empower yourself so that you can influence others to achieve your objectives — is a necessary component of the COE and forms the basis of a compelling argument for the union of CQ and SOF.

Part I of this book underscores the challenges and the solutions to the problems that plague states and their militaries in the contemporary operating environment. Global insecurity in the twenty-first century is discussed, followed by the case supporting SOF as the force of choice for the COE, and the argument for CQ as the tool of choice. Part II flows logically from this contextual information and describes CQ in detail, while Part III develops the SOF-CQ interface. As with all powerful tools and weapons, there is a responsibility to apply CQ ethically. As such, Part IV tackles the ethical considerations of employing cultural intelligence.

In sum, this book provides a compelling argument for empowering SOF, the "force of choice," with CQ, arguably the "tool of choice" in the contemporary operating environment. Moreover, the volume provides not only the rationalization and justification for CQ as an important force enabler and multiplier, but also the means of training and educating SOF in its use. Although written specifically for SOF, the contents of this book apply equally to any military or governmental agency operating in the COE.

PART 1

The Contemporary Security Environment: Challenges and Solutions

Chapter 1

Global (In)Security

Global security or, perhaps more accurately, global insecurity, in the twenty-first century is not simply a linear continuation of the problems that plagued the world during the preceding hundred-year period. While individual aspects of the contemporary operating environment (COE), such as the use of terror as a tactic and the reliance on alliances and coalitions to achieve common goals, are not unprecedented, the COE is markedly different from conflict during much of the twentieth century. Enabled by globalization and the proliferation of the media, and fuelled by the global power vacuum that the end of the Cold War created, the twenty-first century brought with it the "perfect storm" of conditions that has now created substantive global instability.

Scholars, military and security analysts, and practitioners in particular, tend to agree that the contemporary operating environment is extremely complex, ambiguous, volatile, dynamic, and exponentially more dangerous than previous periods. The enemy is no longer limited to symmetrical, uniformed rivals aligned to one of two superpowers. Rather, our adversaries run the gamut of rogue states, regional rivals or power blocks, warlords, globally networked transnational criminals, narco-traffickers, as well as radical extremists fuelled by ideology and/or religion.

Arguably, the concurrent end to the Cold War and the rise of globalization in the 1990s created the conditions that were ripe for the ambiguous, complex, volatile, and ever changing operating environment in which we now find ourselves. With the collapse of the Berlin Wall in 1989, which symbolized the end of the Cold War as a result of the implosion of the Warsaw Pact and the Soviet Union, the rigidly controlled bipolar world tumbled into a free fall. An economic and political power vacuum was created as the superpowers disengaged from many areas around the world. Very quickly, failed and failing states mushroomed around the globe. Exacerbating the situation were other significant problems such as ethnic violence, narco-trafficking, transnational crime, and competition for resources. At the same time, the world was becoming more interconnected or "globalized," as demonstrated by an increase in international traffic, both economic and cultural, linking peoples of disperse geographic regions and thereby redefining power relationships and enabling the proliferation of non-state actors on the world stage.[1]

Certainly, throughout the 1990s the security operating environment continued to become more challenging for Western nations. With only a single global superpower, the United States, the West, following the lead of the Americans, began a series of selective interventions. In this context the landscape for militaries also dramatically changed. The belligerents were no longer clearly identified or well understood. Indeed, operations in the 1990s contained a monumental leap in complexity. Antagonists ranged from military to paramilitary forces, from warlords to criminal organizations and gangs to armed mobs. In addition, military forces had to deal with other governmental departments and agencies, non-traditional coalition partners, non-governmental organizations (NGOs), civilian populations, and an aggressive, omnipresent media.

By 1993, United States Marine Corps (USMC) commandant, General Charles Krulak, described operations in the new security environment within the context of the "three block war." He described an operational concept in which soldiers conducted operations spanning humanitarian assistance to peacekeeping and/or midintensity combat all in the same day and all within three city blocks.[2] Central to Krulak's thinking was the realization that military personnel could no longer rely on the conformity and relative order of the Cold War; they now have to be capable of operating in an ambiguous, chaotic, volatile, and dynamic battleground. Military leaders and soldiers have to operate and conceptualize in non-traditional, non-Western ways and actually think from the perspective of the enemy. Moreover, they need to be able to seamlessly transition through the entire spectrum of conflict to fight the "three block war" all in the same relative area, all in the same day.[3]

Just as militaries began to cope with this new environment the 11 September 2001 terrorist attacks on the twin towers of the World Trade Center in New York (9/11) shattered any level of comfort that they may have developed. A "Global War on Terror" quickly engulfed the Americans and their international allies in deadly struggles in Afghanistan, Iraq, and other parts of the globe. The new adversaries also acted as catalysts to redefine the contemporary operating environment by underscoring existing problems and opening the gates to new challenges. The tactics they adopted, which were applied in the economic, informational, military, societal, and political domains, forced Western industrialized nations to examine how they viewed the world and how they could effectively provide domestic and global security and stability.

Undeniably, the events of 9/11 exacerbated regional instability around the world. In its aftermath, with American and allied focus drawn to Iraq and Afghanistan, many nations found themselves short of the manpower and money, not to mention political will, required to focus as effectively as they may have otherwise been able to in other areas of the world. Consequently, political, military, and social instability continues to increase in certain areas, particularly less affluent regions. Urbanization, resource scarcity, transnational criminal activity, climate change, and pandemics are but a few examples of factors that continue to contribute to regional instability.

Regional instability is an important component of the contemporary operating environment because these areas are often targeted by adversaries of the West in order to harness more strength and support. These troubled areas provide the potential for resources (e.g., recruiting, natural resources that can be exploited for money) and offer sanctuary (to organize, plan, and train). Indeed, weak and failing states prove easy victims to tactics of persuasion and coercion

19

by adversaries. Regardless of their motivation — be it economic, political, or religious — adversaries intent on imposing their political, ideological, or religious will in areas that are already marked by regional instability are difficult to contain because of a lack of political and/or security infrastructure in these areas. Either through corruption, support by rogue states, or force of arms, these fragile states or areas become the breeding ground for global instability. As the Western industrialized world is preoccupied with their ongoing conflicts, already overextended by their current military commitments or simply uninterested in specific regions, the threats proliferate. Regional instability represents a global threat.

However, dealing with the adversaries that have arisen is not a simple task. Those who have faced the overwhelming economic, technologic, and military superiority of the Americans and their allies, or those who have learned the lesson of those confrontations, have realized that success lies in the asymmetric approach. In simple terms this means that our adversaries utilize methodologies in conflict and war that are fundamentally different than that of the opposition to achieve their goals. Respected American strategist Steven Metz explained that asymmetry:

> is acting, organizing, and thinking differently than opponents in order to maximize one's own advantages, exploit an opponent's weaknesses, attain the initiative, or gain greater freedom of action. It can entail different methods, technologies, values, organizations, time perspectives, or some combination of these ... [and it] can have both psychological and physical dimensions.[4]

Colin Gray, another internationally renowned strategist, lamented, "Difficult to respond to in a discriminate and proportionate manner, it is of the nature of asymmetric threats that they are apt to pose a level-of-response dilemma to the victim." He explained, "The military response readily available tends to be unduly heavy-handed, if not plainly irrelevant, while the policy hunt for the carefully measured and precisely targeted reply all too easily can be ensnared in a lengthy political process which inhibits any real action."[5]

But that is the appeal of an asymmetric approach. After all, it is a concept based on the premise of "circumvent[ing] or undermin[ing] an opponent's strengths while exploiting his weaknesses, using methods that differ significantly from the opponent's usual mode of operations."[6] Asymmetric warfare, in contrast with traditional warfare, refers to operations that do not rely on troop numbers or weapons to destroy and/or control an enemy and gain control of an area of operation. Rather, "asymmetric warfare most commonly refers to warfare between opponents not evenly matched where the smaller or weaker force must exploit geography, timing, surprise, or specific vulnerabilities of the larger and stronger enemy force to achieve victory."[7] As Colonel Bernd Horn articulates, "[A]t its core, asymmetry is not designed to win battlefield victory. Rather its aim is to disrupt, distract and disconnect. In short, its goal is to wear down a normally superior opponent."[8]

The reliance on the asymmetric approach as a central tenet of the contemporary operating environment is wrapped up with the concept of fourth generation warfare (4GW), which "refers to a nonlinear approach to conflict and war in which agility, decentralization and initiative are instrumental to success." As part of 4GW, adversaries employ the full range of economic, informational, political, societal, and military capabilities in order to erode an adversary's power, influence, and will. In essence, 4GW "seeks to convince the enemy's political decision makers/political leaders that their strategic goals are either unachievable or too costly for perceived benefit." The struggle "is rooted in the fundamental precept that superior political will, when properly employed, can defeat greater economic and military power."[9] In essence, the enemy uses 4GW in order to influence and affect the non-military population of a country or region. It is "war amongst the people," according to General Sir Rupert Smith.[10]

The concept of 4GW is also important because it captures the ambiguity, complexity, and dynamic nature of the contemporary operating environment. Now the enemy is not necessarily another state. Rather, adversaries are often non-state actors such as al Qaeda or other networked organizations that are capable of significant and deadly operations far removed from their traditional zones of operation. Importantly, the definition of combatants and non-combatants in accordance with internationally accepted conventions and laws of armed conflict are not recognized by many of the adversaries. In fact, to our newly defined enemies "civilian and military is often indistinguishable."[11]

As a result, much of their targeting and attacks do not adhere to the same set of "moral" guidelines and imperatives as those of Western nations. In fact, they often specifically target civilians. The use of terror as a tactic by contemporary adversaries of the West underscores the asymmetry of the contemporary battlefield and the reliance on 4GW.[12] As the events of 9/11 showed, and as developments in Afghanistan and Iraq demonstrate, the use of terror on civilian populations is a powerful tool. It can convince populations to withdraw political support from their governments and force changes in their foreign policy and/or it can coerce populations to cease support of government or coalition forces. It also creates the illusion of strength for the antagonists and utter vulnerability and helplessness on the side of the security forces. As such, terrorism has become a hallmark of the contemporary operating environment.[13]

In fact, terrorism is arguably one of, if not the, dominant theme in the news. Some extremist networks (e.g., al Qaeda) have arguably evolved from an organization with specific goals to an ideology that fuels and attempts to sustain a global terror campaign. In this process, they will continue to reject state sovereignty and ignore borders as well as human rights. Furthermore, recognizing that these practices are unacceptable to the Western way of war, they will continue to hide behind international conventions and national laws when it is to their advantage.[14] In essence, they are operating under a different cultural construct of war and leveraging the cultural restraints of the West — particularly as they pertain to war being viewed as a sanctioned use of force between *nation-states*, as well the sanctity afforded to civilians in times of limited war — in order to further their objectives.

Many adversaries are willing and able to adapt their circumstances as situations dictate. For example, even though suicide bombing is categorically against Pashtunwali, the Afghan moral code, it has become a hallmark of the war in Afghanistan.[15] As such, the COE is in a state of constant change, adding to its complexity and volatility.

Compounding these problems is the fact that our adversaries have both virtual and physical sanctuaries and havens. Through the use of modern, affordable technologies they are able to develop networks and cells that can plan and share finances, information, intelligence, and ideology without ever physically compromising fellow members and they can do so from diverse regions around the world. Moreover, these virtual networks can be in a constant state of change as they adapt to evolving circumstances and recruit from a seemingly limitless pool of Internet users. Terrorist cells can grow, divide, proliferate, and separate, as well as act independently of each other.[16]

The success of these networks will be a function of their effective exploitation of globalization, as well as the proliferation of affordable technology to enhance their capacity and reach. Globalization and access to cheap, easy to use technology will also allow these networks to share lessons learned and tactics, techniques, and procedures (TTPs), thereby evolving in complexity and sophistication. They will grow from a "collective" experience thus becoming more capable and more dangerous.[17]

Moreover, these networks will be hard to identify in the physical world as they lurk through cyberspace, picking up followers and hiding under the Western ideology of nation-state borders and international and national laws. The threat will also become increasingly insidious as "homegrown" terrorists, radicalized on the Internet or in extremist institutions within modern industrialized states, lash out at their "own" societies.[18]

Significantly, their message is often resounding as a multitude of media sources spread news, propaganda, and sensationalism through a variety of outlets on a continuous basis. Indeed, as has been previously noted, "Repeated often enough or pervasively enough, perception becomes reality."[19] And the tactics of the weak and desperate often transform adversaries into unstoppable titans in the eyes of the public, as terrorist attacks are replayed on the evening news for days in full, gory, superficial detail.

This raises another omnipresent, complicating reality of the COE — the ever-present media. Instantaneous reporting from operational areas around the world transforms actions on the ground into pictures in living rooms, often irrespective of context. As a result, seemingly innocuous acts, or even unsubstantiated reports, of individual military personnel can have significant strategic significance if broadcast around the world and viewers take offence.[20] One need only think of the images of the American serviceman being dragged through the streets of Mogadishu, Somalia, in 1993 and the impact that had on the former American President Bill Clinton's administration's foreign policy, or the one paragraph story in *Newsweek* magazine that reported mere allegations of rumours that American guards destroyed copies of the Quran at Guantánamo Bay, which sparked riots and killings around the globe for weeks, to gauge the power of the media to influence attitudes and behaviours.[21]

Importantly, within this complex, volatile, dynamic, and dangerous operating environment, Western nations and their adversaries recognize that the centre of gravity for operational success is the support of the societies in which they operate. Quite simply, people are the "prize." Winning the support of the populace is pivotal for both sides of a conflict as it ensures the long-term success or failure of a campaign, whether seen through the eyes of the state, coalition, insurgent, or terrorist. This connection is easy to understand.

First, citizens provide the necessary will to sustain conflict and to wage war. People control the cultural construct of war by placing limits on what is acceptable to achieve a desired end. They determine how much national blood and treasure can acceptably be expended.

They delineate what levels of violence, collateral damage, and moral standing are acceptable when conducting operations. They determine the political will for governments and politicians. And, whether at home or in the country where operations are taking place, without the support of the people, conflict becomes unsustainable.

Second, the population provides cover and concealment. Adversaries can hide among the people, melting into populated centres and use society's wider anonymity to cloak movement, sustainment, and/or operations. This makes differentiation of friend and foe extremely difficult, allowing adversaries a high degree of freedom of movement and increasing the likelihood of collateral damage by government or coalition forces with the corollary negative impact that has on winning popular support, both at home and in the host nation.

Third, it is access to the population that provides the source of critical information central to developing or denying the necessary intelligence picture required to prosecute operations against an adversary.[22] Advanced technology is a force enabler and modern intelligence, surveillance, and reconnaissance (ISR) assets provide modern industrialized militaries with a dramatic advantage. However, the air campaign against the Serbs in Yugoslavia and Kosovo, as well as operations in Iraq and Afghanistan, clearly demonstrated that clever utilization of ground, particularly in urban areas, stymie even the best ISR platforms.[23] Moreover, technology is unable to accurately measure enemy intent. As such, people provide human intelligence (HUMINT) that can provide the necessary information to generate intelligence driven operations.

Fourth, the people represent resources, either in the form of manpower, shelter, food, and material or the denial of the same. As such, to win the hearts and minds of the populace represents an important source of sustainment, information, and material. Conversely, failure to win the trust and confidence of the people means these vital enablers are at best denied to all belligerents, at worst provided to the enemy.

As many scholars, theorists, and practitioners have demonstrated, popular support of the people is a vital factor in creating the conditions essential for success in the contemporary operating environment. Although this is not a new revelation, or it should not be for those who have studied conflict and war, it is the recent counter-insurgencies in Iraq and Afghanistan that have caused militaries to place increased, if not a totally new, emphasis on the varying cultural constructs of conflict and war, as well as the asymmetric approaches their enemies adopt. It is this axis between Western nations and their adversaries that underscores the fact that conflict and war, as an extension of politics — whether associated with a nation-state or transnational groups — is won or lost in the political arena, not necessarily on the battlefield.

History has repeatedly demonstrated that tactical victory does not equate to strategic triumph.[24] Admittedly, the ability to project military power is often correlated with success but, notably, victory in battle does not necessarily translate to strategic achievement. In the end, success is ultimately dependent on the people's endorsement and acceptance of the conduct, legitimacy, and ultimate outcome of conflict and war. This is true both with regards to the domestic population as well as the host nation citizenry. After all, "people are the prize." They must be convinced to support a specific side or at least not aid an adversary. Indeed, at the turn of the twenty-first century, Thierry Cambournac, head of the French Army's doctrine and combat development bureau, commented on the challenges in future stability operations, "the population constitutes a principal actor in conflicts, and that is a totally new factor."[25]

Clearly, the challenges for Western industrialized militaries operating in the labyrinth of complexity that is the contemporary operating environment are monumental. As people become central to the struggle so does the cultural asymmetry of the combatants and the societies in which they operate. Military personnel must be conscious of their cultural surroundings at home and abroad. After all, to operate effectively in the COE is intimately and inextricably linked to popular support of the respective populations. If a military loses the support of the people due to perceptions that the method of conduct, cost and/or legitimacy of the conflict is unacceptable, then the government and the military institution will ultimately fail.[26] The contemporary operating environment rests on the hearts and minds of affected populations. As a result, it exists as much along the abstract continuum of culture as it does along and within the concrete borders of nation-states, making people the source of power and "the prize" in modern conflict and war. Indeed, in his retirement speech, U.S. Army General P.J. Schoomaker reminded his audience, "We must never forget that war is fought in the human dimension."[27]

Importantly, Westerners are not bystanders in the contemporary operating environment, nor have they ever been; rather, their action and inaction impacts the defence environment on a continuous basis. Thus, understanding the complexities of the contemporary operating environment is a lesson in understanding "self" as well as "other."

In the end, to be successful in the contemporary operating environment means more than just equipping and training soldiers to fight with the most advanced technology and weapons systems available. It requires military personnel who are well trained and equipped, but also well educated. It demands individuals who are not only capable, but who thrive in ambiguity, complexity, and change. It necessitates leaders and soldiers who can anticipate, adapt, and change in accordance with circumstances and situations. But equally, if not more importantly, it demands military professionals who are culturally astute, who can see reality through the eyes of others and utilize that knowledge to influence others to achieve their aims. Only by fully understanding others is it possible to win their trust and confidence and influence them in a substantive lasting way.

Chapter 2

The Force of Choice: Special Operations Forces

The fundamental nature of the contemporary operating environment, (i.e., it being complex, volatile, dynamic, and dangerous) creates the need for forces that are well positioned to meet the challenge of an uncertain and ever-changing, potentially lethal environment. The ambiguous nature and asymmetric conditions that the contemporary operating environment entail position special operations forces as the force of choice because of their highly trained personnel, and their ability to deploy rapidly and apply special skills sets in a variety of environments and circumstances to achieve surgical precision non-kinetic and kinetic effects in peace, conflict, or war. Moreover, despite SOF's focus on technologically advanced equipment, its philosophical and practical adherence to its core strength — namely its emphasis on cognitive responses to ambiguous and complex situations and reliance on individuals who are adaptive, innovative, and agile — make it the ideal counter to an uncertain contemporary and future battle space that is won or lost in the human dimension.[1]

This connection is easier said than done. Special operations forces have always been an enigma to the general public and even their military brethren. Nonetheless, they have been both admired and loathed. Much of this emotion is a result of ignorance and misunderstanding, some of which is the result of the often overly secretive nature of SOF forces. For example, Hollywood, popular literature, and occasional media sound bites and articles have been responsible for much of how SOF is depicted and understood by the public and general military population. These accounts range from the portrayal of a few hard, determined men capable of daring, desperate missions and superhuman feats of martial prowess — the SOF operator being the very epitome of both masculinity and military expertise — to the other end of the spectrum that feeds perceptions and myths of out-of-control misfits and rogues who shun military decorum and discipline and act as a law unto themselves.

The truth about SOF lies some place in between. Understanding these perceptions, myths, and their root causes, as well as the evolution of SOF and its current doctrine is important to understanding SOF and the CQ interface. It is thus necessary to lay a solid foundation of SOF theory, evolution, and doctrine before examining the importance of CQ to SOF and mission success.

SOF BACKGROUND

Constant Themes

In many ways the unique attributes and characteristics of SOF also create vulnerabilities. Their elite status, uniqueness, and definable difference from the conventional military have always created a friction and a kind of barrier between the two entities.[2] In essence, throughout the relatively short history of SOF there have been constant themes that highlighted the cultural and philosophical chasm between the conventional military and SOF. These themes are important to grasp in order to properly understand SOF, as well as for SOF to understand the animosity, if not hostility, they often face from those on the outside.

The subject of SOF never fails to elicit emotional responses from those who partake in the debate. Detractors argue that SOF are "expensive, independent, arrogant, out of uniform, [operate] outside normal chains of command, and [are] too specialized for [their] own good."[3] Major-General Julian Thompson, commenting on the explosion of SOF in the Second World War, captured the essence of the traditional argument when he stated, "descending on the enemy, killing a few guards, blowing up the odd pillbox, and taking a handful of prisoners was not a cost-effective use of ships, craft and highly trained soldiers."[4]

In the same vein, renowned military analyst and author Tom Clancy observed that SOF "units and their men are frequently seen as 'sponges,' sucking up prized personnel and funds at the expense of 'regular' units."[5] In essence, the criticisms and enmity are long-standing. They are also based on constant themes that revolve around competition for scarce resources, return on investment, concepts of discipline and accountability, and a distinct difference in cultural and philosophical methodologies.[6]

Competition for Resources — "Skimming the Cream"

The military is rarely a priority for government spending. As such, nothing fuels animosity and institutional infighting more than the competition for scarce resources. Quite simply, resources allow for organizational expansion, modernization, and training. In Machiavellian terms, they dictate effectiveness, power, and status. However, they are always in short supply and their distribution is always carefully guarded. Not surprisingly, from the inception of SOF units, these newcomers were seen as interlopers that not only siphoned off scarce manpower, but also equipment and money.

No issue engenders animosity between conventional forces and SOF more than the "poaching" of manpower. It is not surprising that commanders are resentful that some of their best officers and men are attracted to, or recruited by, SOF units. "Almost invariably the men volunteering," historian Philip Warner explained, "are the most enterprising, energetic and least dispensable."[7]

The "poachers" themselves conceded as much. "In the first place, there is probably quite a bit of understandable jealousy that any newly formed unit should be given priority as to men and equipment," Major-General David Lloyd Owen, the commander of the Long Range Desert Group (LRDG), acknowledged. He added, "It is only the normal reaction of any good commanding officer to resent

31

having his best men attracted to such 'crackpot' outfits."[8] For this reason, Field Marshal Sir Alan Brooke, Chief of the Imperial General Staff, criticized special operations forces. He argued they were "a dangerous drain on the quality of an infantry battalion."[9]

Field Marshal Viscount Slim agreed. These units he insisted "were usually formed by attracting the best men from normal units by better conditions, promises of excitement and not a little propaganda.... The result of these methods was undoubtedly to lower the quality of the rest of the Army, especially of the infantry, not only by skimming the cream off it, but by encouraging the idea that certain of the normal operations of war were so difficult that only specially equipped corps d'élite could be expected to undertake them."[10]

The issue has not changed with time. In the period immediately following the Second World War, Lieutenant-Colonel J.P. O'Brien charged SOF "ate up far too many junior leaders who were badly needed in the infantry battalions."[11] Similarly, former serving Canadian officer and historian John A. English observed that Moshe Dayan's emphasis on expanding the Israeli airborne force during his tenure as Chief of Staff detracted from the effectiveness of the Israeli infantry as a whole by lowering the quality of soldier entering the standing force Golani Brigade.[12] Clancy also noted that "a private in an airborne unit might well be qualified to be a sergeant or squad leader in a regular formation."[13]

To exacerbate this problem, SOF units most often utilize a higher proportion of senior non-commissioned officers (NCOs). This utilization has the result of reinforcing the claim that the quality of the army suffers from the deficiency of good NCOs due to SOF requirements[14] This argument has also been a core argument of the Canadian Army as its aggressively resists the transfer of its manpower to Canadian Special Operations Forces Command subordinate units such as the Canadian Special Operations Regiment (CSOR) and the Canadian Joint Incident Response Unit (CJIRU).

Return on Investment

The perception of poaching is contentious, but what exacerbates the negative perception even more is the belief held by many that the "return on investment of scarce resources" is wasteful. Field Marshal Slim protested during the Second World War that "the equipment of these special units was more generous than that of normal formations."[15] Similarly, historian Philip Warner observed, "Special forces are often the subject of envy, dislike and misunderstanding because they are ... issued with equipment which is often more lavish than that provided to their parent units."[16]

This is a timeless complaint. General Fred Franks acknowledged the special consideration given to SOF particularly with regards to the expansion of American SOF in the mid-1980s, specifically the Rangers. "As an elite force [Rangers] they were given ample training budgets, stable personnel policies (less rotation in and out than normal units), their pick of volunteers, and leaders and commanders who were already experienced company commanders."[17]

Whether justified or not, many conventional commanders resent the investment of valuable, highly skilled, scarce manpower, combined with the lavish consumption of material resources, particularly since they feel SOF fails to provide a worthwhile return for the costs incurred. The efforts of special units were often likened to "breaking windows by throwing guineas (gold coins) at them."[18] What has historically grated many of the critics is the belief that SOF receives the best personnel and overly generous funding despite spending less actual time in combat. What further exacerbates the negative impression held by the conventional military is that when SOF does undertake combat operations, their casualty rates are usually higher than the average suffered by conventional forces.

A brief overview of SOF operations would appear to confirm these criticisms. However, they do not discount SOF's value to operational success. In almost all cases conventional forces would have been unable to complete the mission or would have required vastly greater resources. After all, most SOF operations are relatively small in terms of manpower. Nonetheless, during the Second World War casualty figures support the thesis that SOF endeavours are indeed risky. For example, the commando raid at Tragino suffered a 100 percent casualty rate; the first SAS raid in North Africa 64 percent; the mission to kill Rommel 96 percent; and the commando landing at Marina, in Italy, 48 percent. For the "greatest raid of all," St. Nazaire, the cost was 79 percent of the commandos and 52 percent of the naval force, who were either killed or captured. British Commandos suffered a significantly higher wartime mortality rate than the rest of their army. The same is true of the Australian commandos, who had a wartime casualty rate of 34 percent.[19] Naval combat demolition units suffered a casualty rate of 52 percent and the First Special Service Force suffered an incredible 78 percent casualty rate in Italy.[20] In the same theatre, during the attempted break-in at Cisterna, only six of the 767 American Rangers who crawled forward in the early morning of 30 January 1944 returned.[21] Across the board, SOF suffered a higher percentage of casualties despite being active in fewer combat situations than actual forces.

Contemporary SOF operations confirm this trend. During Operation Eagle Claw, the attempt to rescue the American hostages in Iran in 1980, all casualties at Desert One were SOF. During Operation Urgent Fury, the invasion of Grenada in 1983, 47 percent of American casualties were SOF and six years later during the action in Panama, Operation Just Cause, the number stood at 48 percent. In 1991, during Desert Storm, SOF casualties represented 17 percent of the total. In the Battle of Mogadishu (1993) it was 62 percent. As of 2003, 63 percent of American casualties suffered as part of Operation Enduring Freedom were SOF.[22] "The commandos [SOF]," one military analyst calculated, "… are statistically nine times as likely to die as regular soldiers…."[23]

Concepts of Discipline and Accountability

While perceptions of preferred manning and wastefulness have created animosity towards SOF, nothing has created more conflict than their perceived lack of discipline and military decorum. To those on the outside, units that do not fit the conventional mould, specifically those described as "elite," "special," or "unique," and that operate with distinct grooming standards, are often criticized as being a "law unto themselves." In fact, sociologist Charles Cotton, in his studies of military culture, noted that "their [SOF/elite] cohesive spirit is a threat to the chain of command and wider cohesion."[24]

The basis of this criticism is rooted in the reality that leadership and discipline are informal within SOF and the normal protocol and emphasis placed on ceremony and deportment are relaxed. Professor Eliot Cohen revealed that "an almost universally observed characteristic of elite [SOF] units is their lack of formal discipline — and sometimes a lack of substantive discipline as well." For example, his research determined that "elite units often disregard spit and polish or orders about saluting."[25]

Cohen was not wrong. General De La Billiere recalled that as a junior officer in the SAS, "The men, for their part, never called me 'Sir' unless they wanted to be rude."[26] Historian Eric Morris noted, "The LRDG and other like units did offer a means of escape from those petty tediums and irritants of everyday life in the British Army. Drills, guards, fatigues and inspections were almost totally absent."[27] Another military historian observed that "[mad Mike] Calvert, [commander 2 SAS Brigade], like many fighting soldiers was not particularly concerned by the trivia of, for example, military appearance [since] uniformity and smartness have little bearing on a unit's ability to fight."[28] But, without a doubt these "trivial" aspects have an enormous impact on how a respective unit is perceived by others, particularly outsiders.

This connection was not lost on the members of SOF units. "We were already conspicuous by our lack of dress code," one SAS noncommissioned officer confessed. "The green army always dresses the same."[29]

One new American special forces operator recalled his amazement on arriving at his new unit. "Sergeants Major are the walking, breathing embodiment of everything that's right in the US Army," he explained. Yet, his first glimpse of his new sergeant-major caught him unprepared. "This guy looked like Joe Shit the Ragman ... His shirt was wide open and he wore no T-shirt. His dog-tags were gold plated. His hat was tipped up on the back of his head, and he wore a huge, elaborately curled and waxed handlebar moustache."[30]

The issue is aggravated by the SOF members, who realize that their lax discipline and dress codes irritate the conventional army. It is part of the SOF appeal, as is their need to clearly differentiate themselves from the "regular" army. This is also why it generates such enmity from the conventional hierarchy.

Much of this dynamic is also based on the type of individuals who join SOF units. David Stirling, the founder of the SAS, reflected that the "Originals" were not really "controllable" but rather "harness-able."[31] The Rangers were acknowledged to consist largely of "mavericks who couldn't make it in conventional units."[32]

"Commanding the Rangers," William Darby, their first commanding officer, explained, "was like driving a team of very high spirited horses. No effort was needed to get them to go forward. The problem was to hold them in check."[33] American Special Forces ("Green Berets") were similarly described as those "who wanted to try something new and challenging, and who chafed at rigid discipline."[34] Furthermore, General De La Billiere observed that, "Most officers and men here do not really fit in normal units of the Army, and that's why they're here in the SAS, which is not like anything else in the Services."[35] He assumed most of the volunteers, like himself, "were individualists who wanted to break away from the formal drill-machine discipline" that existed in the army as a whole.[36] This example fits into a larger pattern. According to General Peter Schoomaker, who joined Delta under its founding commander Colonel Charlie Beckwith, "Beckwith was looking for a bunch of bad cats who wanted to do something different."[37]

SOF, however, is more than just the results of combing a group of self-selecting, "type A," action-oriented individuals. The selection process itself generates cohesiveness. The feeling of accomplishment, as one of the few who has successfully passed selection; and the self-confidence born from challenging and hazardous training creates an aura of invincibility and an intense loyalty to what is perceived to be a very exclusive group.

An intimate bond is further generated through shared hardship and danger. Members of these "special" groups frequently develop an outlook that treats those outside the "club" as inferior and unworthy of respect. Often this sense of independence from the conventional army, as well as the lack of respect for traditional forms of discipline, spawn what some analysts describe as the emergence of units that are more akin to militant clans than military organizations.[38] Needless to say, this type of organization and institutional attitude is an anathema to a military that prides itself on decorum, tradition, and uniformity.

Not surprisingly, the arrogance and deliberate insubordination of some SOF operators fuels the fire of their numerous critics. No image is more representative than the scene in *Black Hawk Down* when a captain gives direction to a group of senior NCOs. Upon completion, the group, less one, acknowledges the orders. The captain quickly confirms with the recalcitrant NCO if he understood the direction. The Delta Force sergeant replies nonchalantly, almost contemptuously, "Yeah, I heard ya." This is a classic example of art reflecting reality.

In another situation, an operator laughingly described how he had failed to salute two "crap-hat" (regular army) captains. He explained that he "couldn't because he was smoking and couldn't do two things at once."[39] In yet another case, a former support officer of a SOF organization revealed, "Assaulters would refuse to listen to others regardless of rank because 'you hadn't done selection.'"[40] Similarly, an executive assistant to a sector commander in Bosnia disclosed that "whenever they [SOF operators] didn't like what they were told they went in to see the commander [and thereby circumvented the chain of command]."[41]

The arrogance and aloofness that can come from the cult of elitism that often exists within groups that are specially selected will create and nurture an "in-group" mentality that becomes dangerous if not controlled by mature, professional leadership. Uncontrolled it can reinforce a belief that they can trust only themselves — that is, those who have also passed the rigorous selection standards and tests.

Anthropologist Donna Winslow confirmed the negative aspects that often arise from an emphasis on the exclusivity of this "warrior cult." It nurtures an unassailable belief that "only those who have done it know, or can be trusted, or more dangerously yet, can give direction."[42] Alan Bell, formerly of the SAS, confessed that they "tended to have an arrogance that we knew it all, did it all, and had nothing to learn." Moreover, he acknowledged that they would work only with Delta Force or SEAL Team Six — no one else. "We figured it wasn't worth our time," he confessed. "We doubted their capabilities."[43]

This type of attitude has consequences. "Too often," observed Tom Clancy, "there's friction, competition, and rivalry — a situation often made worse by the sometimes heavy-handed ways of the SOF community."[44] This reluctance to work with others, compounded by arrogance, breeds animosity, mistrust, and barriers to co-operation and sharing of information with outside agencies. Everyone loses.

Divergent Cultural and Philosophical Methodology

Competition for scarce resources and disagreement on comportment and discipline are not the only basis for conflict, disagreement, and antagonism towards SOF. These elements only support the larger issue — the divergent cultural and philosophical methodologies of SOF and the conventional army. General Leslie Hollis captured the essence of the debate when he stated that there is a misconception within the conventional army that special formations are "a lot of resolute but irresponsible cutthroats, who roam around the campaign area, spreading confusion amongst their own troops and consternation amongst those of the enemy."[45]

A large degree of the problem between SOF and the conventional military stems from the limited and restrained philosophical understanding of war, particularly SOF and its role in the larger context. M.R.D. Foot, a Second World War intelligence officer for the SAS and British historian, stated that special operations "are unorthodox coups ... unexpected strokes of violence, usually mounted and executed outside the military establishment of the day."[46] For those trapped in a conventional, doctrinal mindset, SOF, almost by definition, become problematic. "To the orthodox, traditional soldier," Colonel Aaron Banks explained, "it [unrestricted warfare] was something slimy, underhanded, illegal, and ungentlemanly. It did not fit in the honor code of that profession of arms."[47] Almost fifty years later, the same sentiment remains. "There is a cultural aversion on the part of conventional soldiers, sailors, and airmen," Lieutenant-General Samuel Wilson explained, "to things that smell of smoke and mirrors and feats of daring-do.... It's a little too romantic.... It's not doing it the hard way."[48]

The nature of war and how it is fought is not the only issue of concern, however. Commanders often likened SOF to "Private Armies," that tend to "become an object of suspicion to the public army."[49] This linkage is often due to the fact that SOF value agility, flexibility, and rapid response — in short, action — and they have little institutional patience for bureaucracy. Coupled with an "ends justifies the means" attitude, it is not surprising that conventional feathers often get ruffled. "One danger of the private army [SOF]," commented one senior officer, "is certainly that it gets into the habit of using wrong channels."[50] He was not alone in his observation. Calvert also conceded that "A private army ... short-circuits command."[51]

This apparent disrespect for the chain of command is not surprising since SOF type units have often owed their existence or survival to a powerful mentor who is well-positioned to look after his wards. For instance, Prime Minister Winston Churchill took great interest in the development of the commandos and he supported other similar aggressive, unorthodox units. General George Marshall personally pushed his subordinates to support the establishment of the American Rangers, and his political master, President Franklin D. Roosevelt, allowed the director of the Office of Strategic Services (OSS) to maintain a direct pipeline to the White House. Later, President John F. Kennedy heaped lavish attention on the American Special Forces, much to the chagrin of his conventional chiefs of staff and, recently, Secretary of Defence Donald Rumsfeld personally ensured that

American SOF received starring roles in U.S. operations, as well as hefty increases in manpower and budgets. Finally, it was no secret that former Canadian Chief of the Defence Staff, General Rick Hillier, was the creator and protector of the Canadian Special Operations Forces Command against vehement internal opposition, particularly within the Canadian Army. It is not surprising that SOF are more than willing to use their special connections to further their cause. This type of special access and privilege infuriates conventional commanders, who try to even the score whenever possible.

The refusal to co-operate or work with conventional forces due to "security concerns" creates another impediment to co-existence. Often SOF operators arrive in theatre to conduct secret missions without informing the "in-place unit" or commanders. Their presence normally generates suspicion with belligerent forces who recognize "new players," as well as potentially negative consequences should SOF action occur. At the end of the normally short operation, the "in-place" force must deal with the brunt of the belligerent reaction. To add insult to injury, the need for "operations security" is normally used as the reason for completely ignoring conventional forces. Yet, paradoxically, the compulsion to ensure that they are easily distinguished from the conventional military seems to override the need for secrecy. In fact, it compels them to use exotic equipment, uniforms, and dress codes completely apart from the normal military patterns, even when not required for operational purposes. The result is that they are easily identified, further exacerbating the rift.[52]

A corollary effect of the exaggerated emphasis on secrecy and refusal to work with conventional forces is that SOF are misunderstood by conventional forces. "I was appalled," former SAS Commander, Major-General Tony Jeapes stated, "by the lack of understanding of the Regiment's capabilities by those in high positions." However, he conceded that the "Regiment's insistence upon secrecy in all it did had become counter-productive."[53] Although operations security is paramount, secrecy in and of itself often becomes a tool to avoid scrutiny and build barriers to the outside world. This inflated cloak of secrecy is not only questionable but, more importantly, is an impediment to progress and contributes to the gulf between SOF and conventional forces.

It is not only cultural practices and overt attitudes that elicit conflict between SOF and conventional forces. There is also a philosophical difference rooted in the type of individuals that are drawn to SOF compared to those who remain in the conventional forces that creates tension between the two groups. "Of course, we're all concerned with people who are different," a former commander of the 75th Ranger Regiment exclaimed. "We are uncomfortable with it ... in particular in the military because it is so structured and when all of a sudden you have unstructured beings, people are not comfortable with them.... We had some people who had tremendous capabilities, tremendous skills, but people didn't want to be around them ...These free thinkers. These people who did things in an unconventional manner."[54] This difference has always been an issue.

Mavericks, critical thinkers, and individuals who can conceptualize innovative tactics, equipment, and methodologies that are alien to the conventional wisdom were, and still are, often marginalized. Yet their ideas and contributions, once properly harnessed and allowed to flourish, provide incredible payback. These attributes are the strength of SOF.

That was evident from the start. "You'd volunteered for the Commandos," one recruit explained, "they realised that you were human beings and you had a bit of sense, that you didn't need to be roared at and shouted at, screamed at all the time ... Not only that, if you did anything, even in training, everything was explained to you. If you'd a different idea, even as a lowly Private, you could say 'Well, sir, don't you think if we went that way instead of this way it would be easier?' If you were right that was the method that was adopted."[55]

An SAS commander explained the concept. "I never had a roll call or kit checks before operations [in Malaya] ... If a man could not look after himself our opinion was that he had no place in the SAS ... The men responded to this trust and never once did I have cause to regret it."[56]

41

That is the philosophy that is so alien to the conventional army but resonates so strongly with SOF. It also underlines SOF's greatest strength and the greatest reason for the chasm between SOF and conventional forces: the individual operators.

SOF Contributions to the Conventional Military

Despite the litany of criticisms, SOF has continued to exist and, in fact, prosper in the post 9/11 era. The reasons for their longevity lie in what SOF actually provides to the military and government they serve.[57]

First, they are extremely cohesive, having with an unquestioned solidarity between their members. In SOF units officers and men undergo identical training and are faced with the same tests of courage, endurance, and strength. Generally, they have all passed the rigorous selection standards. In short, there are no shortcuts and no distinctions for anyone. As a result of the exacting standards and shared hardships, a bond is created based on group identity, mutual respect, and solidarity. Membership in the fraternity cannot be bestowed due to affluence, connections, or rank. It must be earned.

Sociologists have argued that high standards and requirements to enter into a group result in a greater sense of commitment and value placed on membership to that group by successful candidates.[58] In simple terms, the greater the degree of challenge, hardship and danger, the greater is the development of mutual respect and affiliation.[59]

These bonds are significant. Samuel Stouffer's monumental study of battlefield behaviour, *The American Soldier*, indicated that 80 percent of respondents believed that a strong group integration was the main reason for stamina in combat. The study also observed that motivation is primarily dependent on group cohesion and that group cohesion is the decisive factor for combat efficiency. The steadfast self-confidence in oneself and one's fellow soldiers engenders a belief and philosophy that there is no mission that cannot be accomplished.[60] As such, SOF units provide a very reliable and effective combat force, regardless of the difficulty of the task.

Moreover, SOF can also be a source of inspiration and set a standard for others. They provide an opportunity and goal for those who wish to challenge themselves and aspire to meet the rigorous selection standards for entry into an elite unit. This opportunity and challenge can act as a catalyst for pushing those in the military to aspire to more challenging work and potentially retaining members who may retire failing to meet the challenge or adventure they were seeking.

SOF units also provide a leadership nursery. Members have the opportunity to learn additional skills, particularly advanced leadership abilities, due to their exposure to different training and operational experiences and more experienced and highly skilled personnel in their own forces and government departments, as well their allies or coalition partners. As these leaders return to their units or are deployed to formations, schools, or various headquarters they share their acquired attributes, insights, and skills. This cross-pollination strengthens the military institution as a whole. For example, SOF leaders have been responsible for enhancing such skills as marksmanship, mentoring, and close quarter battle drills (CQB) within combat arms units.

SOF units are also a preferred testing ground for new tactics, techniques, and procedures, as well as technology. SOF units usually represent smaller, more experienced and talented organizations. Additionally, they often operate in very small teams. For those reasons it is easier to test new processes, TTPs, or technology within SOF and then refine them prior to transferring skills to the wider organization. Within Canadian SOF alone the impact has been dramatic. Canadian SOF have been responsible for a number of important evolutions in army equipment and tactics — specifically in the realm of load bearing vests, communications equipment, sniper rifles equipment, close quarter battle drills, and joint tactical air control techniques and procedures, to name a few.

But the greatest contribution of SOF, particularly in the contemporary environment, is the flexibility and range of strategic options they provide the most senior military commanders and their political masters. A large part of this senior level support comes from their being privy to what SOF actually accomplish and getting to work side by side with the members of the various elite units as well as their leadership. For them, many of the misperceptions that are prevalent elsewhere do not exist because they are not only aware of the results that are achieved, but they actually provide the necessary direction and approval for the actual missions. As such, the questionable "return" on investment is not an issue. They are fully aware that their SOF units "punch above their weight" and deliver results far in excess of the numbers engaged. For instance, few realize that Canadian SOF has removed an entire generation of Taliban leadership in Kandahar, many of whom were responsible for the deaths of Canadians.

For those not privy to this level of information, the veil of secrecy still exists, which inevitably breeds misconception and misunderstanding. However, SOF units consciously err on the side of caution with regard to overexposure rather than attempt to showcase their successes. This is due to two moral imperatives. The first is the requirement to protect their personnel who operate against a ruthless enemy in an unforgiving, complex operational environment. The second is to protect operations to ensure mission success, which also includes the essential requirement to protect allies and their information and TTPs.

Equally, the intimate dealings of senior decision makers with members and leadership of SOF units exposes them to the overriding humility and professionalism normally present in military personnel. This is not to say that exceptions do not exist — clearly they do, as they do in any organization. Overall, however, a quiet confidence and maturity normally permeates SOF organizations. Senior journalist and Harvard scholar Linda Robinson observed that the SOF forces she has worked with were "largely self-policing because senior members usually detect and address breakdowns in a soldier's performance." She added, "There is a high level of intolerance among [the group] for performance that falls short of the standards and there are also the checks of peer competition with other teams and oversight by the hierarchy above."[61] The greatest fear and punishment is banishment, or in simplest terms, "RTU" — return to unit of origin.

But the greatest reason for maintaining SOF organizations is the capability they provide the government: a panoply of options (kinetic and non-kinetic) not available elsewhere. Specifically, this includes agile, tailored, rapid responses to high-risk situations. These organizations are often charged with "no fail" tasks. Their training, expertise, high readiness levels, and specialized equipment position them to deter, disrupt, and/or defeat enemy threats in the manner least disruptive and damaging to the society they serve. If they fail the government is left with little space in which to manoeuvre. The only possible alternative would be to send in a large kinetic force and to deal with its ensuing footprint and consequence — an option that is sometimes not possible and most often not desirable.

Certainly, the importance of their success is also why SOF are often provided with generous budgets and cutting-edge technology. To counter a determined enemy that is networked and ever changing, as well as a myriad of threats in a complex environment, it is not enough to simply react. Ultimate success depends on staying ahead of the threat environment. For this reason, a heavy investment in a nation's "no fail" force is often taken to ensure they maintain the necessary capabilities that are required when a crisis arrives.

SOF THEORY[62]

Having discussed the underpinning of the consistent themes that have generated animosity, if not a chasm, between the conventional military and SOF, it is important to examine the foundational tenants of SOF theory. The starting point is the actual definition of SOF.

Defining SOF — Exactly Who or What Are SOF?

SOF means many different things to many different people. They have been defined based on a myriad of concepts ranging from: units and organizations that do "special" activities; units that perform tasks or roles not done by conventional units; and units that conduct actions behind enemy lines. Journalists usually define SOF as "the toughest, smartest, most secretive, fittest, best-equipped and consistently lethal killers in the U.S. [or any other] military."[63] However, a more traditional definition spawned from SOF's Second World War and immediate postwar beginnings describes them as forces that are "specially selected, specially trained, specially equipped, and given special missions and support."[64]

For the basis of this study, SOF will be defined in accordance with the Canadian doctrinal definition:

> Special Operation Forces are organizations containing specially selected personnel that are organized, equipped and trained to conduct high-risk, high value special operations to achieve military, political, economic or informational objectives by using special and unique operational methodologies in hostile, denied or politically sensitive areas to achieve desired tactical, operational and/or strategic effects in times of peace, conflict or war.[65]

Special People — The SOF Edge

In the aftermath of 9/11 and the resultant global war on terror, SOF have become the "force of choice" of most modern nations to fight the shadowy and wily terrorists, insurgents, and other non-state actors. However, the effectiveness and success of SOF are not exclusively contingent on the special equipment, cutting-edge technology, or even the special training of SOF personnel. The key factor to SOF success, as mentioned, is its people. CANSOF, like its international brethren, equip the operator rather than man the equipment.

The special people who self-select, the individuals who are attracted to SOF, and those who are ultimately chosen to serve in SOF are what provide the SOF edge — the ultimate ingredient for mission success.

Self-selection is not enough. In the case of Canadian Special Operations Forces Command (CANSOFCOM), each of its four units have a unique mandate, thus each unit has a set of distinctive requirements for its personnel, be they operators, specialists, or supporters.[66] To aid in selecting the right person for these different positions, several distinct screening and/or selection processes exist across and within CANSOFCOM units. These processes have been scientifically derived and are based on job analyses that identified specific attributes required of personnel in order to be successful on the job in the SOF environment. For some jobs the screening and selection processes are fairly straightforward, comprised of a file review, background check, interview, and psychological screening. More elaborate selection processes (i.e., assessment centres) exist for the more specialized and demanding SOF roles.

The assessment centre is a process used to measure a predetermined set of job-related competencies in-groups of individuals and is typically comprised of a collection of structured assessment instruments such as interviews, simulation exercises, and teamwork events, all of which are measured by multiple trained assessors. The actual construction and content of the respective assessment centre varies depending on organizational mandate, hence the requirement for separate and distinct assessment centres for the different CANSOFCOM units.

In the end, to achieve the SOF edge that provides the catalyst for success, SOF organizations seek individuals who are:

1. *Risk Accepting* — Individuals who are not reckless, but rather carefully consider all options and consequences and balance the risk of acting versus the failure to act. They possess the moral courage to make decisions and take action within the commander's intent and their legal parameters of action to achieve mission success.

2. *Creative* — Individuals who are capable of assessing a situation and deriving innovative solutions, kinetic or non-kinetic, to best resolve a particular circumstance. In essence, they have the intellectual and experiential ability to immediately change the combat process.

3. *Agile Thinkers* — Individuals who are able to transition between tasks quickly and effortlessly. They can perform multiple tasks at the same time, in the same place, with the same forces. They can seamlessly transition from kinetic to non-kinetic or vice versa, employing the entire spectrum of military, political, social, and economic solutions to complex problems to achieve the desired outcomes. They can react quickly to rapidly changing situations, transition between widely different activities, and ensure they position themselves to exploit fleeting opportunities. Moreover, they can work effectively within rules of engagement (ROE) in volatile, ambiguous, and complex threat environments and use the appropriate levels of force.

4. *Adaptive* — Individuals who respond effectively to changing situations and tasks as they arise. They do not fear the unknown and embrace change as an inherent and important dynamic element in the evolution of organizations, warfare, and society.

5. *Self-Reliant* — Individuals who exercise professional military judgment and disciplined initiative to achieve the commander's intent without the necessity of constant supervision, support, or encouragement. They accept that neither rank nor appointment solely define responsibility for mission success. They function cohesively as part of a team but also perform superbly as individuals. They continue to carry on with a task until it becomes impossible to do so. They take control of their own professional development, personal affairs, and destiny and strive to become the best possible military professional achievable. They demonstrate constant dedication, initiative, and discipline and maintain the highest standards of personal conduct. They understand that they are

responsible and accountable for their actions at all times and always make the correct moral decisions regardless of situation or circumstance.

6. *Eager for Challenge* — Individuals who have an unconquerable desire to fight and win. They have an unflinching acceptance of risk and a mindset that accepts that no challenge is too great. They are tenacious, unyielding, and unremitting in the pursuit of mission success.

7. *Naturally Orientated to the Pursuit of Excellence* — Individuals who consistently demonstrate an uncompromising, persistent effort to excel at absolutely everything they do. Their driving focus is to attain the highest standards of personal, professional, and technical expertise, competence, and integrity. They have an unremitting emphasis on continually adapting, innovating, and learning to achieve the highest possible standards of personal, tactical, and operational proficiency and effectiveness.

8. *Relentless in Their Pursuit of Mission Success* — Individuals who embody a belief that service to country is first and foremost before self. They have an unwavering dedication to mission success and an acceptance of hardship and sacrifice. They strive to achieve mission success at all costs, yet within full compliance of legal mandates, civil law, and the law of armed conflict.

9. *Culturally Attuned* — Individuals who are warrior/diplomats, who are comfortable fighting but equally skilled at finding non-kinetic solutions to problems. They are capable of operating individually, in small teams, or larger organizations integrally or with allies and coalition partners. They are also comfortable and adept at dealing with civilians, other governmental departments (OGDs), and international organizations, as well as non-governmental organizations (NGOs). They are culturally attuned and understand that it is important to "see reality" through the eyes of another culture. They understand that it is not the message that was intended that is important but rather the message that was received that matters. They strive to be empathetic, understanding, and

respectful at all times when dealing with others. They comprehend that respect and understanding build trust, credibility, and mission success.

SOF Capabilities

SOF are a strategic asset that provides governments with a wide range of kinetic and non-kinetic options to pre-empt, disrupt, react, or shape national efforts domestically or abroad. Key to the employment of the full spectrum of SOF options is the timely engagement of SOF by decision makers to advise, plan, and deploy in a timely manner. Quite simply, time equals options. SOF are capable of providing the government:

1. High readiness, low profile, task-tailored special operations task forces (SOTFs) that can be deployed rapidly over long distances and provide tailored proportional responses to a myriad of different situations.
2. Highly trained and capable, technologically enabled forces that can gain access to hostile, denied, or politically sensitive areas.
3. Discrete forces that can provide discriminate surgically precise kinetic and non-kinetic effects.
4. A deployed capable and internationally recognized force, yet with a generally lower profile and less intrusive presence than larger conventional forces.
5. An economy of effort foreign policy implement that can be used to assist coalition and/or allied operations.
6. A rapidly deployable force that can assess and survey potential crisis areas or hot spots to provide "ground truth" and situational awareness for governmental decision makers.
7. A highly trained, specialized force capable of providing a response to ambiguous, asymmetric, unconventional situations that fall outside the capability threshold of law

enforcement agencies (LEAs), conventional military or OGDs.

8. A force capable of operating globally in austere, harsh, and dangerous environments with limited support. SOF are largely self-contained and can communicate worldwide with organic equipment and provide limited medical support for themselves and those they support.

9. A culturally attuned SOTF or teams that can act as a force multiplier through the ability to work closely with regional civilian and military authorities and organizations, as well as populations through defence, diplomacy, and military assistance (DDMA)/security force assistance initiatives.

10. A force capable of preparing and shaping environments or battle spaces (i.e., setting conditions to mitigate risk and facilitate successful introduction of follow-on forces).

11. A force capable of fostering inter-agency and inter departmental co-operation.

SOF Truths

SOF operations over the years have generated five internationally accepted and espoused SOF "Truths" that speak to the nature of SOF and special operations.

1. *Humans are more important than hardware.* The SOF operator is the "core system" and the reason for mission success. In essence, SOF equips and enables the man; it does not man the equipment.

2. *Quality is better than quantity.* This truth is self-explanatory. In the end, effectiveness and special operations mission success is normally more dependent on the presence of qualified, specially trained, and experienced operators who are agile in thought and action, culturally attuned and adaptive, as well as creative in their response to changing, complex, or

ambiguous situations than it is on the number of actual boots on the ground.

3. *SOF cannot be mass produced.* The special selection and subsequent training, education, and experience that is accumulated over time through the necessary practice, exercise, and operations to create the fully mature, insightful, reflective, and capable SOF operator takes time, as well as dedicated resources and mentorship. There are no shortcuts or methodologies for increasing output.

4. *Competent SOF cannot be rapidly created after emergencies occur.* A solid SOF capability with depth of personnel and capacity requires a consistent, well-resourced structure that continually nurtures and grows the SOF capability, and looks to the future to ensure constant evolution to not only be capable of reacting to and defeating the next threat but pre-empting and disrupting it. SOF must always stay ahead of a nation's adversaries. Without this consistent long-range outlook, the ability to quickly generate the necessary SOF capability or increased capacity is impossible in the immediate aftermath of a crisis. It will take time to create/develop/grow the necessary SOF response after the fact if it has not been anticipated, supported or resourced prior to the emergency.

5. *Most Special Operations require non-SOF assistance.*[67] Despite SOF's attributes and characteristics SOF relies on conventional forces to assistance in most of its mission sets either through supporting functions, particular combat enablers (e.g., airlift, fires, Intelligence, Surveillance, Reconnaissance [ISR], intelligence), or with combat forces (e.g., cordon and/or follow-on forces).

Factors for Successful SOF Employment

Historically, a common SOF criticism of conventional commanders has been their inability to properly employ SOF forces assigned to them. The following factors assist in ensuring the successful employment of SOF elements:

1. Clear national and theatre strategic objectives.
2. Compartmentalized knowledge of SOF tasking, planning, and mission execution in accordance with strict operations security (OPSEC) guidelines and the principle of "the need to know."
3. Effective command, control, communications, computers, and intelligence (C4I) support at all levels.
4. Realization that SOTF are most effective when they are fully integrated into the joint/theatre task force commander's (TFC) overall campaign plan. SOF employment is nested in the superior commander's intent and SOF actions remain visible and transparent to those who need to know.
5. Appropriate mission/tasks sets. SOF should only be employed against targets with strategic or operational significance. Improper employment could result in the unnecessary wastage of SOF. They cannot be quickly replaced or reconstituted, nor can their capabilities be rapidly expanded. SOF are not a substitute for conventional forces. In most cases SOF are neither trained nor equipped to conduct sustained conventional combat operations, and should not be substituted for conventional units that are better able to effectively execute a conventional mission.
6. Decisive early and timely engagement of SOF to emerging situations will act as a force multiplier for decision makers as it will increase the number of options they will have to deal with the possible crisis. Simply put, the earlier the notice of a potential mission, the greater the likelihood of effective employment (e.g., preposition assets) and successful effects. In essence, decision makers can inadvertently eliminate the SOF option by failing to enable them to be in the right place at the right time.
7. Comprehension that SOF logistic support is austere in nature and geared toward the requirements of fielding and

supporting rapidly deployable and agile forces, not the extended support of fielded forces.

CANSOFCOM DOCTRINAL COMPONENTS

SOF IN THE CF CONTEXT

On 19 April 2005, the Chief of the Defence Staff declared that he planned "on bringing JTF 2, along with all the enablers that it would need, to conduct operations successfully into one organization with one commander."[68] As a result, on 1 February 2006, as part of the CF's transformation program Canadian Special Operations Command was created. The purpose of CANSOFCOM is to force develop, generate, and, where required, force employ special operations task forces (SOTF) capable of achieving tactical, operational, and strategic effects required by the Government of Canada (GoC).

CANSOFCOM Vision

The CANSOFCOM vision is to be an agile, adaptive, and high-readiness special operations force capable of providing scaleable kinetic and non-kinetic response to missions of strategic significance to the Government of Canada.

CANSOFCOM Mission

The command mission states: "CANSOFCOM will provide the government of Canada with agile, high-readiness special operations forces capable of conducting special operations across the spectrum of conflict at home and abroad."

CANSOFCOM Tasks

CANSOFCOM is responsible for:

1. Providing the Government of Canada with high readiness special operations forces capable of conducting:
    a. Counter Terrorism (CT) Operations — offensive and defensive measures taken to prevent, deter, pre-empt, and respond to terrorism;
    b. Maritime Counter-Terrorism (MCT) Operations — CT operations within the extremely complex maritime environment; and
    c. High Value Tasks (HVT) — other missions, at home or abroad, kinetic or non-kinetic, that may be assigned by the Government of Canada such as: special reconnaissance (SR); direct action (DA); counter proliferation (CP); non-combatant evacuation (NEO) and defence, diplomacy, and military assistance (DDMA).[69]

2. Force generating and deploying special operations forces capable of global reach and response to emerging threats to Canada's national interest;

3. Force development of SOF forces and organizations that remain on the leading edge of technology and operational capability to meet the requirements of the current and future security environments;

4. Providing expert advice on special operations and CT to government officials, other government departments (OGDs), senior military decision makers and other CF entities for routine planning, exercise or crisis events;

5. Providing the GoC and the CF with a conduit to allied special operations and CT expertise, technology, research and development; and

6. Contributing to strengthening the CF by offering a challenging and dynamic career opportunity that will attract members to join the CF and remain for a rewarding career.

Solving the People Puzzle

Operational Imperatives

CANSOFCOM has developed a number of operational imperatives that are key to achieving their tasks and which, combined with their personnel, form the foundation of their "SOF edge." They are the basic operational tenets that Canadian special operations forces hold as fundamental to achieving mission success. Ultimately, it is the man, not the equipment or technology that prevails and assures victory, particularly in the face of complexity, chaos, and confusion. It is the ascendancy of an indomitable warrior spirit that fuels the "SOF edge." The operational imperatives are:

1. *Relentless Task and Mission Focus* — an unwavering commitment to mission success.
2. *Adherence to the Highest Uncompromising Standards* — an unyielding and resolute personal commitment to achieve and maintain the highest standards of personal and organizational competence tradecraft and conduct.
3. *Flourish in Conditions of Ambiguity and Chaos* — an acceptance that operations will always be conducted in a context of potential, if not perpetual, ambiguity, chaos and change.
4. *Interoperability* — the realization that the battle space is complex, dynamic, and interconnected by a myriad of organizations and capabilities that must be coordinated, fused, and integrated to achieve the best possible effect and mission success.
5. *Operations Security* — the recognition that security is a fundamental prerequisite for SOF.

Ethos and Core Values

The CANSOFCOM ethos is a direct subset of the Canadian Forces military ethos. As such, it is an amalgam of the values, beliefs, and expectations that reflect core Canadian values, the imperatives of service in CANSOFCOM and the requirements of special operations. It is the underpinning of CANSOF professionalism and establishes an ethical framework for the professional conduct of all of CANSOF operations. Moreover, the ethos acts as a unifying spirit that encompasses all members of CANSOFCOM. It clarifies how CANSOFCOM members view their responsibilities, apply their expertise, and express their unique military identity. It serves to shape and guide their conduct and encompasses values that define their professional conduct. In essence, it is the foundation upon which the legitimacy, effectiveness, and honour of CANSOFCOM depends and it represents the undying commitment of CANSOF members to each other.

The CANSOFCOM ethos is captured through the expression of its Core Values:

1. *Internalization of CF Core Values* — this entails understanding, accepting, and internalizing the four core values of the CF, which are fundamental to CANSOFCOM members as Canadians and practitioners of the profession of arms. Specifically the CF values as interpreted by SOF are:
    (i) **Duty** — entails first and foremost service to country before self; unwavering dedication to mission success; acceptance of hardship and sacrifice; compliance with law and adherence to the law of armed conflict; maintenance of the highest levels of tactical and technical competence; audacity in accepting personal risk for mission accomplishment; the relentless pursuit of excellence in the execution of all tasks; constant dedication, initiative, and discipline; maintenance of the highest standards of personal conduct; being responsible and accountable for your actions at all times; and always making the correct moral decisions regardless of situation or circumstance;
    (ii) **Loyalty** — entails unquestioned allegiance to country and faithfulness to comrades; the dedicated

support of the intentions of superiors and obedience to lawful direction and commands; the strength to question and challenge decisions and directives when required (truth to power); and the adherence to the two moral imperatives of mission success and the safety and well-being of your subordinates;

(iii) **Integrity** — entails the unconditional and steadfast commitment to a principled approach to meeting your obligations; being trusted with the most sensitive missions and information; maintaining the nation's values; operating to the highest moral standards and always being responsible and accountable for your actions regardless of situation or circumstance. It requires transparency in actions and honesty in word and deed within the constraints of operations security and the tenet of "need to know"; and

(iv) **Courage** — entails willpower and the resolve not to quit; an uncompromising and unrelenting drive to overcome all obstacles and achieve mission success; an overwhelming desire to fight and win; it requires individuals to disregard the cost of an action in terms of physical difficulty, risk, discomfort, advancement or popularity; and it enables individuals to make the right choices among difficult alternatives. SOF demands the uncompromising moral and physical courage under all conditions.

2. *Relentless Pursuit of Excellence* — entails an uncompromising, persistent effort to excel at absolutely everything we do; the consistent and driving focus at attaining the highest standards of personal, professional and technical expertise, competence, and integrity; the unremitting emphasis on continually adapting, innovating, learning to achieve the highest possible standards of personal, tactical, and operational proficiency and effectiveness.

3. *Indomitable Spirit* — entails the unconquerable desire to fight and win; the acceptance of risk; a mindset that accepts that no challenge is too great; a tenacious, unyielding, and unremitting pursuit of mission success; and a disregard for discomfort.

4. *Shared Responsibility* — entails the exercising of professional military judgment and disciplined initiative to achieve the commander's intent; an acceptance that neither rank, nor appointment define sole responsibility for mission success; the requirement for everyone to contribute to the plan, conduct and execution of a task through collaborative planning, innovative ideas, feedback, the sharing of expertise and competence; and the unwavering loyalty and support of those entrusted with a task or command. This includes the responsibility of "Truth to Power," that is the requirement to address shortcomings in ability, experience or training whether it is found in subordinates, peers or superiors.

5. *Creativity* — entails the realization that innovation, the agility of thought and action, as well as inventive, unconventional solutions to unexpected problems are the only response to a battle space that is exponentially more complex and chaotic, as well as rife with ambiguity, uncertainty and change; as well as the rejection of risk aversion or a reliance on status quo traditional responses to new, unique or changing circumstances.

6. *Humility* — entails an adherence and dedication to quiet professionalism; a personal commitment to the highest standards of professionalism; and it focuses on serving a higher authority — the nation and the people of Canada.

In the larger CF institutional context, CANSOFCOM contributes to the defence of Canada through its integral support to the six core *Canada First Defence Strategy* missions:

1. **Conduct daily domestic and continental operations, including in the Arctic and through NORAD.** CANSOFCOM can deploy agile, tailored, rapidly deployable SOTFs able to

provide a wide range of SOF operations capabilities and to operate in an independent, joint or integrated context in any environment including urban and harsh, remote locations.

2. ***Support a major international event in Canada, such as the 2010 Olympics.*** CANSOFCOM offers the GoC and the CF a wide range of SOF capabilities that both support and enhance law enforcement agencies (LEA) and conventional military forces.

3. ***Respond to a major terrorist attack.*** CANSOFCOM is the CF lead for counter-terrorism response both domestically and abroad.

4. ***Support civilian authorities during a crisis in Canada such as a natural disaster.*** CANSOFCOM offers the GoC and the CF rapidly deployable self-contained SOTFs that have integral communications, as well as a high degree of mobility and medical support.

5. ***Lead and/or conduct a major international operation for an extended period.*** CANSOFCOM is globally focussed to help shape the operational environment to support and enhance the conventional military and campaign plan and the whole of government approach.

6. ***Deploy forces in response to crises elsewhere in the world for shorter period.*** CANSOFCOM is capable of rapidly deploying task-tailored SOTFs and/or small teams capable of fulfilling a wide range of SOF functions that allow the GoC accurate timely situational awareness, as well as the widest possible number of response options.

In the more general sense, CANSOFCOM fully participates in the primary CF mission of providing for the defence of Canada, particularly counter-terrorism. Its forces are organized, equipped, and trained not only to be responsive but also to serve as a deterrent. Through interagency liaison, discussion, and training, CANSOFCOM seeks to enable and assist other government departments where appropriate in CT planning and execution.

CANSOFCOM also contributes to the overall defence of Canadian national interests by conducting operations abroad in support of CF conventional forces, as well as on discrete missions that support GoC objectives. CANSOFCOM provides strategic flexibility to tailored responses in a complex strategic environment. The high readiness posture, skill level, and deployability of its SOTFs allow for a rapid and determined response, but also serve as a building block and/or shaping force for follow-on forces when necessary. CANSOFCOM provides forces that can deter and disrupt adversaries either in support of conventional operations or on discrete missions. CANSOFCOM forces may also assist partners in upgrading their CT capabilities.

SOF Effects in the Domestic Theatre

CANSOFCOM fully participates in the primary CF mission of providing for the defence of Canada. Specifically, it is capable of delivering the following operational and strategic effects:

- **Operational Effects**
  - Assist, Establish, and Maintain Arctic Security
  - Organize, Enable, and Improve Forces Available to Conduct Surveillance
  - Persuade or Deter Others from Inappropriate use of Canadian Territory
  - Disorganize, Disrupt, Degrade or Deny Others from the use of Canadian Territory.
- **Strategic Effects**
  - Defend Canada
  - Defeat Terrorist Threats in Canada
  - Provide CT Forces Capable of Operating in All Environments
  - Provide Crisis Response Forces for Weapons of Mass Effect Incidents

- o   Deter Terrorist Activity in Canada
- o   Enable and Assist Other Government Departments

SOF Effects in Out of Area Operations

CANSOFCOM also contributes to the overall defence of Canadian national interests by conducting operations abroad in support of CF conventional forces and on discrete operations that support GoC objectives. CANSOFCOM provides strategic flexibility by way of specifically tailored response options to a wide range of complex issues in the strategic environment. Of note, CANSOFCOM is capable of delivering the following operational and strategic effects abroad:

- **Operational Effects**
  - o   Organize, Enable, and Improve Partners Tactical and Operational Skills
  - o   Destroy, Disorganize, and Disrupt the Networks of Adversaries
  - o   Degrade and Deny Access of Adversaries to Populations
  - o   Construct Social Networks to Promote Legitimacy of Efforts
- **Strategic Effects**
  - o   Enable Partners to Improve Their SOF Skills
  - o   Erode Support for Violence Orientated Conflict Resolution
  - o   Deter and Disrupt Adversaries
  - o   Shape Environment for Follow-On Forces
  - o   Provide Flexibility in Strategic Environments

The complex, volatile, dynamic, and dangerous contemporary operating environment has highlighted the requirement for agile, effective forces that are resourced, trained, and empowered with leading edge equipment, technology, and training methodologies.

Most importantly, the COE also demands forces that are cognitively capable of assessing and dealing with challenging situations, especially those that arise from cultural ambiguities and/or differences. The COE requires a force that is able to leverage capabilities such as CQ through cognitive development. In turn, these tools act as force multipliers because they maximize the ability to acquire the assistance of those best able to provide insight and intelligence to a specific conflict or component thereof. As such, this brief overview of SOF background, theory, and a specifically CANSOFCOM doctrinal baseline has been provided to frame the discourse that follows.

Chapter 3

The Tool of Choice:
Cultural Intelligence

It's all cultural in the end.
— Lieutenant-Colonel Ian Hope,
Commanding Officer Canadian Battle Group
(Task Force Orion)[1]

An American veteran of several foreign interventions once observed of the U.S. military, "What we need is cultural intelligence ... What I [as a soldier] need to understand is how these societies function. What makes them tick? Who makes the decisions? What is it about their society that is so remarkably different in their values, in the way they think compared to my values and the way I think?"[2]

More recently, Brigadier-General David Fraser, the former commander of the International Security Assistance Force (ISAF) Multi-National Brigade Sector South in Kandahar, Afghanistan, admitted, "I underestimated one factor — culture." He elaborated, "I was looking at the wrong map — I needed to look at the tribal map not the geographic map. The tribal map is over 2,000 years old. Wherever we go in the world we must take in to account culture. Culture will affect what we do. This is the most important map [i.e., tribal] there is.... I did not take that in up front. Not all enemy reported was actually Taliban — identification of enemy forces was often culturally driven."[3] In fact, retired U.S. Major-General Robert H. Scales explicitly described how in the contemporary operating environment, military victory "will be defined more in terms of capturing the psych-cultural rather than the geographical high ground."[4]

As argued in Chapter One, in the contemporary operating environment, the seminal battle is often about influencing the population to support the governing authority and deny support and information to the antagonists. To have any hope of influencing the masses and, especially, to win their hearts and minds, it is vitally important to understand them and their culture. Failure to understand their beliefs, values, and attitudes and how they "see" the world is tantamount to mission failure. Sorting out the people puzzle is critical to success. As such, cultural intelligence[5] — or the ability to recognize the shared beliefs, values, attitudes, and behaviours of a group of people and apply that knowledge toward a specific goal — is one of the, if not *the*, key mission enabler in the COE. As Major Ben Connable of the U.S. Marine Corps appropriately noted, "Failure to refocus … on sustainable culture programs will lead to another wave of first-round operational failures."[6] Retired French Colonel Henri Bore recognized that "operational culture is a combat skill that is critical to mission success."[7]

The Importance of CQ to the COE

The non-linear and asymmetric approach of the contemporary operating environment, particularly with respect to insurgencies and counter-insurgencies, demands that soldiers act as warriors and technicians as well as scholars and diplomats. Kinetic solutions are no longer the panacea of warfare. Individuals need to see through the eyes of another culture, specifically the one with which they are interacting, to adapt their attitudes and behaviours in order to better influence the target audience to achieve specific aims. Cultural knowledge contributes to this, while an understanding of CQ and, in particular, the four CQ domain paradigm, provides a fluid template for how to use cultural knowledge to attain desired objectives.[8] Failure to do so can be disastrous. As military experts Jacob Kipp, Lester Grau, Karl Prinslow, and Don Smith argue, "Conducting military operations in a low-intensity conflict without ethnographic and cultural intelligence is like building a house without using your thumbs: it is a wasteful, clumsy, and unnecessarily slow process at best, with a high probability for frustration and failure ... while waste on the building site means merely loss of time and materials, waste on the battlefield means loss of life, both civilian and military, with high potential for failure having grave geopolitical consequences to the loser."[9]

The *Marine Corps Small Wars Manual* warned, "Human reactions cannot be reduced to exact science, but there are certain principles that should guide our conduct ... Psychological errors may be committed which antagonize the population of a country occupied and all the foreign sympathizers; mistakes may have the most far-reaching effect and it may require a long period to re-establish confidence, respect, and order."[10]

As Philip Taylor, professor of International Communications at the University of Leeds, U.K., noted, "In a generational war of ideas, the two key elements to winning are credibility and trust. These take time to create and cultivate, to show potential adversaries what kind of people we really are, that indeed we are not their enemies."[11]

The ongoing conflicts in Afghanistan and Iraq underscore the importance of exhibiting high CQ in the contemporary operating environment, especially during counter-insurgency campaigns. For example, in his retirement speech, U.S. Army General P. J. Schoomaker reminded his audience, "We must never forget that war is fought in the human dimension."[12]

Similarly, Lieutenant-Colonel Ian Hope, a combat tested Canadian battle group commander in Afghanistan remarked, "In combat, the power of personality, intellect and intuition, determination and trust, outweigh the power of technology, and everything else."[13]

Testifying to the House of Armed Services Committee, retired U.S. Army Major-General Robert H. Scales commented on the

> difficulties that would be encountered during the present "cultural" phase of the war [Iraq] where intimate knowledge of the enemy's motivation, intent, will, tactical method and cultural environment has

> proven to be far more important for success than the deployment of smart bombs, unmanned aircraft and expansive bandwidth ... success in this phase rests with the ability of leaders to think and adapt faster than the enemy and for soldiers to thrive in an environment of uncertainty, ambiguity and unfamiliar cultural circumstances.[14]

These two theatres of conflict also highlight that people are the prize in the COE. As Kipp and his colleagues note, "From the varied examinations of the historical record of insurgency is a broad consensus that civil society in Iraq and Afghanistan — as in past insurgencies — constitutes the real center of gravity."[15] Notably, as Benjamin T. Delp, assistant director for policy and administration at the Institute for Infrastructure and Information Assurance at James Madison University, recognizes, these connections are best made prior to entering into conflict. "While high ranking military officers and commanders on the ground have only recently begun to recognize the importance of ethnographic and cultural intelligence for success in Iraq, decision-makers in Washington D.C. must understand the value of analyzing foreign populations' cultural identities prior to, during, and after U.S. military intervention for current U.S. objectives to be realized."[16]

Retired American General Anthony Charles Zinni described the turbulent and chaotic environment modern military personnel would face on operations. "The situations you're going to be faced with go far beyond what you're trained for in a very narrow military sense. They become cultural issues; issues of traumatized populations' welfare, food, shelter; issues of government; issues of cultural, ethnic, religious problems; historic issues; economic issues that you have to deal with that aren't part of the METT-T [mission, enemy, troops, terrain, and weather — time available] process necessarily. And the rigid military thinking can get you in trouble. What you need to know isn't what our intel[ligence] apparatus is geared to collect for you and to analyze and to present to you."[17]

Arguably, the ongoing conflicts in Afghanistan and Iraq have served as a "wake-up call" to Western militaries "that adversary culture matters." While many soldiers serving in conflict zones realize this, the message needs to percolate to higher echelons and be "actioned" accordingly. As a returning U.S. commander from Iraq noted, "I had perfect situational awareness. What I lacked was cultural awareness. I knew where every enemy tank was dug in on the outskirts of Tallil. Only problem was, my soldiers had to fight fanatics charging on foot or in pickups and firing AK-47s and RPGs [rocket-propelled grenades] ... Great technical intelligence. Wrong enemy."[18] This comment caused cultural anthropologist Montgomery McFate to note, "understanding one's enemy requires more than a satellite photo of an arms dump. Rather, it requires an understanding of their interests, habits, intentions, beliefs, social organizations, and political symbols — in other words, their culture."[19] McFate continued to argue that "culture matters operationally and strategically ... misunderstanding culture at a strategic level can produce policies that exacerbate an insurgency; a lack of cultural knowledge at an operational level can lead to negative public opinion; and ignorance of the culture at a tactical level endangers both civilians and troops."[20] Conversely, she also noted, "Understanding adversary culture can make a positive difference strategically, operationally and tactically."[21] McFate concluded that, "The more unconventional the adversary, and the further from Western cultural norms, the more we need to understand the society and underlying cultural dynamics. To defeat non-Western opponents who are transnational in scope, nonhierarchical in structure, clandestine in approach, and who operate outside the context of nation-states, we need to improve our capacity to understand foreign cultures."[22]

These "truths" are not lost to the men and women who are serving in conflict zones. As one American veteran of Iraq realized, "American military culture interacts with Iraqi Isalmic culture like a head-on collision ... massive deployments of American soldiers fighting a counter-insurgency now hurts more than it helps. When we focus on the military solution to resolve a social problem, we inevitably create more insurgents than we can capture or kill. As a consequence, the real 'Islamic terrorists' subverting their own tolerant religion will use this popular anger and sense of resentment to their advantage."[23]

A common theme that surfaces in the accounts of soldiers serving in conflict zones is the need for a deeper understanding of host nation peoples. "The pitfalls presented by a different culture and an ill-defined, poorly functioning (or non-existent) local judicial, administrative, and political systems are enormous," Major P.M. Zeman of the United States Marine Corps noted.[24]

American Naval Reservist, Lorenzo Puertas, commented, "Every war is a war of persuasion … we must destroy the enemy's will to fight…. Persuasion always is culturally sensitive. You cannot persuade someone if you do not understand his language, motivations, fears, and desires."[25]

In fact, many in the U.S. military argue that "a fresh look at IO [information operations[26]] and the military's focus on perception management is crucial to success in one of the key strategic elements of the Global War on Terror: the battle to persuade the Iraqi and Afghan peoples that their future lies in the establishment of a democratic, non-fundamentalist society."[27]

Regrettably, General Thomas Metz, who from May 2004 to February 2005 commanded the Multi-National Corps — Iraq (MNC-I), acknowledged, "The truth of the matter is that our enemy is better at integrating information-based operations, primarily through mass media, into his operations than we are." He elaborated, "In some respects, we seem tied to our legacy doctrine and less than completely resolved to cope with the benefits and challenges of information globalization. We are too wedded to procedures that are anchored in the Cold War industrial age."[28] An anonymous source from inside the Pentagon echoed those sentiments, "We've got to stop trying to 'out-religion' these people and we need to stop looking for a purely military solution to this insurgency [Iraq]. We need to give IO officers and commanders comprehensive cultural training so they can tailor the right message to the Iraqi people."[29]

However, this type of education and training cannot be limited to the upper ranks in the military. After all, in this global age of media, decisions by soldiers in remote areas can have far-reaching consequences for home and host populations. As French Colonel Henri Bore observed, "Knowledge acquired does not depend on rank but on mission, task, and military occupational speciality."[30]

American Naval Reservist, Lorenzo Puertas illustrates this point by describing the potential consequences of one corporal and his decisions after being fired on in an alley in Iraq. "Without cultural training, his reaction will be a product of his personal experiences and beliefs ... He might have cultural misunderstandings that lead to serious errors in judgement. He might fail in his mission — and he might find himself despised by one poor neighbourhood, or by a billion horrified TV viewers." Puertas cautioned, "Cultural knowledge of the battle space should not be left to on-the-job training."[31] Indeed, it has been noted that, "In the constant cross cultural exchange a simple mistake could become an obscenity without the 'guilty' party even being aware of the error."[32]

The fact is, in the contemporary operating environment everyone down to the lowest ranking individual requires cultural intelligence. In the CNN era of 24/7 instantaneous news coverage that beam events as they happen into the living rooms of audiences around the world, the careless act of a single soldier can have strategic ramifications. With regard to the concept of the "strategic corporal"[33] Canadian Colonel Bernd Horn observed, "The perception of the media, as well as that of defence analysts, right or wrong, for better or for worse, is critical ... They [the media] set the terms of the public debate. What they report becomes the basis of societal perception; it influences and forms the public's attitudes and beliefs. Repeated often enough or pervasively enough, perception becomes reality." Thus, Horn concluded that militaries "must always be attentive and responsive to the perceptions of others."[34] Therefore, in the COE, which is almost always in the glare of international media,

71

everyone who participates must be culturally savvy to ensure they do not purposefully or inadvertently offend or alienate audiences at home, abroad, or in the operational area.

Errors concerning cultural sensitivity can have grave consequences for the individual as well as the mission. As Lieutenant-General Andrew Leslie, a former deputy commander of the International Security Assistance Force (ISAF) revealed, "Individuals were sent home [from Afghanistan]. Immaturity and the inability to actually think outside the box made them ineffective … What they tried to do was bring their usually very limited experience from somewhere else and apply it the same way that it had been done somewhere else and that didn't work … each mission has got it's own unique drivers, cultural conditions, local nuances, relationships with your other allies or other combatants."[35]

Despite the obvious need for cultural knowledge and an understanding of how best to apply this knowledge to further the mission, there is nonetheless a gap in knowledge and application of these skills among military personnel. As Major-General Scales pointed out, the U.S. military has a big gap in cultural intelligence. "It is not just a matter of getting more linguists … Rather, and more importantly, there is a need to get your point across — including intent — and in order to do this cultural appreciation is paramount."[36]

Without question there is an immediate need for high levels of cultural intelligence in the contemporary operating environment. In order to help fill this gap in knowledge one must first understand what culture is, as well appreciate how the concept of cultural intelligence came into being. Then one needs a useful, flexible template on which to hang culturally specific knowledge so that it may be used to fulfill military objectives.

PART II

Cultural Intelligence In-Depth

Chapter 4

Making Sense of the Cultural Quagmire

It is important to conceptualize cultural intelligence in such a way as to provide a useful template upon which to hang cultural specific information. CQ is a concept that hinges on the idea of culture. The issue of culture itself is fraught with academic debate. Yet, to fully understand CQ, one must first make sense of this academic quagmire.

The literature is replete with various description and definitions of culture. It is a concept that anthropologists and other academics have long analyzed and debated, yet there remains no clear consensus as to its definition.

The most important thing to understand about culture is its sheer complexity. As Lieutenant-Colonel Ian Hope, commanding officer of the Canadian Battle Group Task Force Orion stated, "It's all cultural in the end."[1] In combination with this epiphany it is crucial to note that our understandings of culture are limited by *our* understandings of the world and are thus susceptible to the fallacies of ethnocentrisms. Nonetheless, in order for CQ to be an effective force multiplier, we need to map the cultural minefield as effectively as possible.

Defining Culture

In basic terms, culture refers to a set of common beliefs and values within a group of people that, combined, transform into attitudes that are expressed as behaviours[2] (see Figure 1). Culture helps to create individual and group identity. Group identity is formed when individuals who share common attitudes and behaviours identify with each other. Individuals may enter into the group already having bought into the shared attitudes and behaviours, or the group may instigate this commonality. Cultural values, beliefs, and attitudes are generally long-lasting and resistant to change. They are passed down through generations and are often unconscious in nature.

BELIEFS + VALUES → ATTITUDE = BEHAVIOUR

Figure 1. The relationships between beliefs, values, attitudes, and behaviours.[3]

Beliefs represent perceived facts about the world (and beyond) that do not require evaluation or proof of their correctness.[4] For example, Pagans believe in many gods, Christians believe in one God, and Muslims believe in Allah. None of these competing religious beliefs has been unequivocally proven correct. Some beliefs may even continue to be held within a group of people in spite of refuting perceived facts. This can lead to cause and effect relationships being misconceived due to the rigidity of a certain belief. For instance, if you believed without question that technology improves quality of life then as technology advanced you would either take it for granted that quality of life was also on the rise or, faced with blatant evidence to the contrary, you would assume that it was not technology that caused this decline. Despite the limitations that certain beliefs place on an individual or group's ability to fully evaluate their surroundings, common beliefs remain at the core of cultural identity.

Values place a moral and/or pragmatic weight on beliefs.[5] For instances, Christians do not simply believe in God, they use this belief to build an understanding of what is important in life. In this sense, Christian values, provide a moral shorthand for determining right from wrong. From a pragmatic perspective, if you believe that university education enables individuals to earn more over the course of a lifetime, and economic advancement is something that you deem important, then you will attach a high worth, or value, to university education.

The relationships between beliefs and values are complex and dynamic. Values are generally attached to beliefs, yet adhering to certain values can also strengthen beliefs or create new ones. Paradoxically, individuals and groups can simultaneously have competing beliefs and values. Often, the weight attached to a certain belief will determine the course of action. For example, a moderate pacifist may be against all forms of violence and also believe strongly in self-preservation and the right to self-defence. In a situation in which the alternatives are shoot or be shot, this pacifist might choose to kill his/her attacker. In the same situation, someone with strong pacifist beliefs may prefer to be shot than go against this belief. What may seem irrational to some can be completely logical to others based on their beliefs and values.

In combination, beliefs and values create attitudes. Attitudes reflect a consistent emotional response to a belief-value pair.[6] To change an attitude, either the belief or its associated value must be altered. To return to a previous example, if you believe that university education increases lifetime earnings and you value economic incentives, then you will have a positive attitude towards higher education. For your attitude toward higher education to change either you must no longer believe that education leads to higher earnings, or the value that you place on economic incentives must be altered. Notably, many belief-value pairs may combine to form, strengthen, or weaken an attitude. To continue with the university education example, in addition to higher earnings you might also believe that a university education allows for more career flexibility, something that you consider to be important to quality of life. Your positive attitude towards higher education would thus be strengthened.

It is important to see attitudes as distinct from simply the combination of beliefs and values because, once formed, they may not be so easily broken down into their component parts and it is attitudes, not just beliefs and values, which predict behaviours. That being said, the best way to alter attitudes is to target their core belief-value pairs with the understanding that there could be several pairs in operation at once. Notably, information and knowledge can help create a shift in attitudes.

Behaviour is the way in which individuals express themselves, be it verbal or non-verbal. In addition to being influenced by attitudes, motivation plays a role in determining behaviour. Motivation can be influenced by the strength of beliefs and values that form attitudes (internal motivation) or it can come from outside of the individual (external motivation), such as bribery, yet the applicability of external influences will also be influenced by beliefs, values, and attitudes. For example, bribing someone with money will only work if that person values money.

Culture is expressed through shared behaviours including language, religion, work habits, and recreation practices. It helps people to classify their experiences and communicate them symbolically. Generally, our daily lives reflect our beliefs, values, and attitudes in a multitude of ways. They shape our lives and contribute to our sense of identity. Culture influences what we do and who we think we are. In parallel, our beliefs, values, and attitudes, as demonstrated through our behaviours, also shape how others see us.

Within a culture, subcultures and countercultures exist. Subcultures, while distinct from their host culture, exist in harmony with it. Thus, individuals can belong to many subcultures within a broader culture. For example, a Canadian can identify with the national culture while at the same time being part of the subcultures of female Canadians; black, female Canadians; and heterosexual, black, female Canadians. All of these subcultures align with the overarching liberal-democratic value system that contributes to Canadian culture yet simultaneously excludes some Canadians. Conversely, countercultures are smaller groups that go against the larger cultural group to which they belong. Fascist-Canadians would fit into this group. The ideologies associated with fascism do not match those expressed by the Canadian Charter of Rights and Freedoms established in 1982. Thus, it is somewhat of a paradox to be both a fascist and a Canadian.

It is only perspective that determines if a group is considered a subculture or a counterculture. The previous example hinges on whether or not you accept that the Charter is illustrative of Canadian beliefs and values and consequently Canadian culture. For some, fascist Canadians would simply be a subculture within the national culture. But most Canadians would likely classify them as a counterculture. It is important to appreciate that perspective plays a key role in this type of interpretation.

The complexity of culture cannot be overstated. Not only do cultures comprise many intertwining layers of meaning, they are living organisms that are, despite their static appearance, in a continuous state of flux. The U.S. Marine Corps handbook on operational culture for deploying personnel to Afghanistan noted, "The study of culture is never 'finished.' What was true yesterday is slowly changing."[7]

In addition to helping individuals make sense of the world, cultures developed as a means of survival.[8] In this way they have geographic and geopolitical roots.[9] Beliefs, values, and attitudes that comprise cultural identity take root in perceptions of the world that are formed based on perceptions about geographic and climatic realities. In his contentious yet thought provoking book about the impeding clash of civilizations, Samuel P. Huntington was perhaps overly simplistic when he stated, "The major differences in political and economic development among civilizations are clearly rooted in their different cultures."[10] Surely, the African continent at large did not choose a culture of poverty. Rather, geography and geopolitics contributed to the development of African culture. In fact, it is more accurate to examine the impact that geography and geopolitics have on culture and vice versa (see Figure 2). Geography and geopolitics influence culture, which in turn shapes geopolitical dynamics and the degree to which geographic features are (or can be) manipulated.

Geography + Geopolitics ↔ Culture

Figure 2. The relationships between geography, geopolitics, and culture.

Geography and geopolitics help cultural groups distinguish themselves from others. Huntington noted, "We know who we are only when we know who we are not and often only when we know whom we are against."[11] He elaborated, "People and nations are attempting to answer the most basic question humans can face: who are we? ... People define themselves in terms of ancestry, religion, language, history, values, customs, and institutions. They identify with cultural groups: tribes, ethnic groups, religious communities, nations, and, at the broadest level, civilizations."[12]

Through this logic, we in the West have come to see the world in terms of us versus them, or "the West versus the rest." This at once presupposes a Western cultural commonality and simultaneously admits that "the rest" (as opposed to East) comprises several non-Western entities.

Even in the "West versus rest" paradigm, states remain the primary actors in the world.[13] This is an important factor to keep in mind because it represents a central paradox in the way that many people see the world. On one hand, nations are grouped according to broad belief-value systems to which the nation-state contributes but that extend far beyond the limits of national borders. On the other hand, our legal frameworks and default understandings remain at the nation-state level. For example, while it is clear that insurgents in the war in Afghanistan are of many national groups and some are finding refuge in Pakistan, the international community can take no legal action within Pakistan's borders.

Self-Identity and Group Identity

Even in the twenty-first century, as national and super-national identities shape global politics it is important to recall that individual humans form the core of cultural identities. Thus self-identity contributes to group identity and vice versa.

Psychologist Abraham Maslow appreciated these connections. In the 1940s he proposed hierarchy of human needs to help explain human motivation. At the base of Maslow's hierarchy are physiological needs such as food, water, and sleep. The second level is safety needs, including security of body, employment, and resources. The third level is feeling loved and belonging to a group. The fourth level is esteem, comprised of self-esteem, confidence, achievement, and respect of and by others. The pinnacle of the hierarchy is self-actualization and has components of morality, creativity, spontaneity, problem solving, lack of prejudice, and acceptance of facts. According to Maslow subsequent phases in the hierarchy can only be reached on achievement of previous base levels. Thus, it is impossible to reach self-actualization if personal safety issues are not resolved.[14]

Maslow's hierarchy is not without fault. For example, suicide bombers give up their basic safety in order to fulfill what they consider to be a higher purpose, or in Maslow's terms, self-actualization. Nonetheless, Maslow's hierarchy has merit as a basic guideline for human motivation. Importantly, for success in the contemporary operating environment, Maslow's hierarchy of needs provides some insight on how to win the hearts and minds of local populations. Certainly, providing basic physiological and safety requirements to host nation (HN) citizens can help them advance along the hierarchy of needs and may influence them to your way of thinking. For example, if coalition forces in Afghanistan provide basic resources and safety to Afghans this may help Afghan citizens identify with being part of the Western international community. It may also help them to disassociate with Taliban insurgents.

Hofstede's Four Value Dimensions

Individuals are the building blocks of culture and can be targeted to create shifts in cultural beliefs, values, attitudes, and behaviours. These transformations need to occur at a group level in order to be beneficial to the Western defence community.

In order to use cultural knowledge to further the mission, the Canadian Forces as an organization needs to be able to identify key aspects about culture that shape beliefs and values, consequently determining attitudes and behaviours. Importantly, the criteria used to assess one culture should be the same as those used to assess other cultural groups.

One way of making sense of the cultural quagmire is by using Geert Hofstede's four value dimensions: power distance, uncertainty avoidance, individualism/collectivism, and masculinity/femininity.[15] It should be noted that a variety of value dimensions exist to help explain group behaviour.[16] These "shortcuts" should not be used as "absolute truths." They should be considered as guidelines that help direct what questions should be asked about cultural constructs that can help further your cause. For the military community, Hofstede's four value dimensions underscore basic areas of culture that are important in the COE.

Notably, while Hofstede's four value dimension model has significant value in providing an understanding within and between cultures, it does not create a black and white dichotomy through which one can easily conceptualize culture. Rather, culture remains hidden beneath layers of complexity. Part of the challenge remains the identity of self versus group, the existence of subcultures and countercultures, the Western tendency to default to national cultures, and the dynamic nature of culture. To illustrate part of this "grey zone," after each description of one of Hofstede's four value dimensions the CF's position on the continuum is provided.

Hofstede's power distance dimension examines the extent to which power between individuals in a group is considered appropriate. For instances, a group with a high power distance quotient would likely believe that order and inequality exist in the world and that everyone has their particular place in the hierarchy. Based on these beliefs they would value a social structure that does not challenge this power distance relationship. Their attitudes would not question the legitimacy of power. Their behaviours would then reflect these attitudes. The caste system in India is just one example. Conversely, societies that score low on the power distance scale believe that all people are created equal. They value social structures that are equalitarian and would only support a government structure that was seen as legitimate, representative of and responsible to the people. Western democracies, and the ideal socialist state, are representative of the types of institutions that would function well in a lower power distance state. With respect to leadership practices, cultures that adhere to a high power distance relationship would likely respond to authoritarian leadership whereas those comprising a low power distance relationship would likely rebel against such unrestrained authority. The latter society would be best led by someone who at least appeared to be more transformational and engaged in consultative leadership.

The CF is, paradoxically, an example of a high power distance group that exists within the low power distance structure of Canadian society. The rank structure of the CF as it upholds the value system of a Western liberal democratic nation is case and point.

The second value dimension that Hofstede describes is uncertainty avoidance. This scale explores the extent to which a culture is challenged by and seeks to avoid situations that are unknown and/or ambiguous. Those societies ranking high on this scale create formal rules that guide behaviours in complex circumstances. These behaviours are rooted in a series of absolute beliefs about the world and their associated values. Dissent from these "truisms" is not tolerated. The Catholic Church for example continues to adhere to creationism versus evolution. Ritualistic behaviour also shows low uncertainty avoidance. Moreover, societal laws and regulations, while created for many reasons, help to maintain low uncertainty avoidance. One can generally accurately predict outcomes based on the adherence to laws and customs; consequences for not abiding by them are sometimes less easily predicted. Societies that are low in uncertainty avoidance are more open to risk and change. Core beliefs can be challenged and attitudes and behaviours duly adjusted. However, this is neither an easy or quick task. Even though cultures are in a continuous state of change, by their very definition they are stable and enduring. Societies that are not happy with the *status quo*, such as failed or failing states, can arguably be categorized as having low uncertainty avoidance.

Again, the CF displays a full range of qualities along this continuum. Guided by a democratically elected government, the CF does not initiate or seek its deployments. In an attempt to maintain global stability, thereby exhibiting high uncertainty avoidance, the Canadian government decides where to send the CF. Once deployed CF personnel need to take initiative and react to complex scenarios that involve multiple players. This demands that CF personnel respond well to situations that are highly unpredictable, volatile, and unstable. Thus they need to behave effectively in situations that are characterised by low uncertainty avoidance.

The next value dimension is that of individualism versus collectivism. Individualistic societies believe that one is responsible for their own well-being. The state or society should not be held accountable or responsible for the welfare of its citizens. Moreover, identity is based on individual achievements and failures, and each person should take the initiative for success. Despite some social welfare systems, American and Canadian societies are prime examples of individualistic societies. Conversely, a collectivist society is organized around the idea that identity is strongly associated with the group and that the individuals that comprise the group have a duty and responsibility to each other to ensure membership well-being and group success. Afghanistan's family, clan, and tribal structure are a good example.

The CF comprises members of a highly individualistic society. Yet, as a group, the CF is highly collective in nature. Indeed, the biggest fear of soldiers deployed overseas is not of dying, it is the fear of letting down their comrades.[17] The cohesion within the CF can be further broken down into unit and subunit levels.

Hofstede's final category of analysis is the masculinity-femininity dimension. This scale reflects the degree to which the principle values in a society reflect stereotypically masculine perspectives, such as competition and aggression, versus those that are stereotypically feminine, such as diplomacy and equality. Societies that identify strongly with stereotypically masculine qualities tend to view the roles of men and women in society as polarized, with men having the dominant position over women. Afghanistan is an example of such a society. Those that prefer feminine attributes tend to consider the roles of men and women as more similar and equal, as we do in Canada.

The CF undeniably has a warrior ethos that demonstrates characteristically masculine traits. Yet, as an organization, it also demonstrates some feminine attributes such as gender equality.

The example of how the CF fits into each of Hofstede's four value dimensions underscores the point that these dimensions are not easily applied to real life. Certainly, actual case studies are impossible to squeeze neatly into each box. Yet, these dimensions do provide insight into some of the ways in which groups see the world. They are useful in providing some basic conceptualizations about culture and establishing categories in which more precise cultural knowledge can be placed. Moreover, at a basic level, Hofstede's four value dimensions can also help you appreciate how others see you.

Cultural understandings are at the core of the ability to exhibit high cultural intelligence. Appreciating some of the basic building blocks of culture is essential when studying CQ. The enigma of culture, however, remains hidden beneath layers of complexity and continuous change that, paradoxically, manifests itself in a stable, long-lasting construct. Human behaviour, at a group level, can be partially explained by shared beliefs, values, and attitudes. Individuals, as the building blocks of cultures, can be targeted to shift cultural beliefs and values, but to win hearts and minds it must occur at a group level. Geert Hofstede's four value dimensions underscore some of the fundamentals that contribute to cultural beliefs and values. Appreciating these value dimensions contributes to an understanding of cultures, both "ours" and "theirs." Additionally, understanding how and along what lines cultures develop and sustain themselves is of critical importance in being able to demonstrate high levels of CQ.

Chapter 5

Defining Cultural Intelligence and the Four CQ Domain Paradigm

CQ is a new label that has been attached to an old concept, leading to the creation of several definitions over the years. Despite the plethora of descriptions of CQ, the term lacks a concise definition, but it is important to establish a practical definition and conceptualization of CQ as it applies to the defence community in order to create a common language and understanding of the concept and its application to the contemporary operating environment.

Despite some fundamental differences between the academic and military literature pertaining to CQ, both the civilian and military schools of thought are inextricably linked and each requires further explanation. One of the leading authors on CQ in the civilian domain is scholar P. Christopher Earley. Earley, working with Elaine Mosakowski in a 2004 *Harvard Business Review* article, described CQ as an outsider's "... ability to interpret someone's unfamiliar and ambiguous gestures in just the way that person's compatriots and colleagues would, even to mirror them ... A person with high cultural intelligence can somehow tease out of a person's or group's behaviour those features that would be true of all people and all groups, those peculiar to this person or this group, and those that are neither universal nor idiosyncratic. The vast realm that lies between those two poles is culture."[1]

In a more complex analysis of CQ, Earley and Soon Ang vaguely defined it as "a person's capability to adapt effectively to new cultural contexts." They further explained that CQ has both process and content features that comprise cognitive, motivational, and behavioural elements.[2] Earley and Randall S. Peterson elaborated on this concept and build upon Earley and Ang's original concept that "CQ captures [the] capability for adaptation across cultures and ... reflects a person's capability to gather, interpret, and act upon these radically different cues to function effectively across cultural settings or in a multicultural situation ... CQ reflects a person's capability of developing entirely novel behaviour (e.g., speech, sounds, gestures, etc.) if required ... At its core, CQ consists of three fundamental elements: metacognition and cognition (thinking, learning and strategizing); motivation (efficacy and confidence, persistence, value congruence and affect for the new culture); and behavior (social mimicry, and behavioural repertoire)."[3]

Other researchers have explored the idea of CQ being composed of cognitive, motivational, and behavioural domains or similar variations of this triplex system. For instance, James Johnson and a group of researchers defined CQ in terms of attitude, skills, and knowledge. Another scholar in the field, David C. Thomas, emphasized knowledge, skills, and mindfulness.[4]

Most of this literature prioritizes CQ as pertaining to other cultures and not one's own. Earley and Ang were clear when they stated, "CQ reflects a person's adaptation to new cultural settings and capability to deal effectively with other people with whom the person does not share a common cultural background."[5] They even went so far as to suggest that individuals who are part of their own cultural in-group would find it particularly difficult to adjust to a new cultural setting as it may be one of the first times that they experience alienation from the in-group and lessons learned in one culture may not be useful in another.[6]

However, this argument ignores the support and reactions of the home population. Although this concept is something that may work for businesses, it is not acceptable for militaries serving democratic nations. The ability of an individual to understand beliefs, values, and attitudes that translate into behavioural patterns of members of their own society must remain an important aspect of the definition of CQ as it applies to the Canadian Forces and other Western militaries. Certainly, most of the military literature that discusses CQ recognizes this fact. For example, Carol McCann, head of Defence Research Development Canada (DRDC)'s adversarial intent section explains, "It's important that if you are going to think about another culture, knowing your own culture and what your norms and values are could be important. If you know you have those things, you're more able to think about operating in a culture you're not familiar with."[7]

To help mitigate problems that arise from cultural misunderstandings and to maximize support at home and abroad for operations, Western militaries, particularly the Americans, are starting to define CQ and underscore important aspects about culture that contribute to mission success. For example, American Army scholar and researcher Leonard Wong and his team describe cultural savvy, or in our terms CQ, for their report to the U.S. Army War College as enabling "an officer [to] see perspectives outside his or her own boundaries." They explained, "It does not imply, however, that the officer abandons the Army or U.S. culture in pursuit of a relativistic worldview. Instead, the future strategic leader is grounded in National and Army values, but is also able to anticipate and understand the values, assumptions, and norms of other groups, organizations, and nations."[8] For their part, the U.S. Center for Advanced Defense Studies defined cultural intelligence along the following lines:

> Cultural awareness is an understanding of all aspects of a nation's *cultural arc* — its past, present, and future. Once awareness is achieved, tools that constantly create such awareness can be incorporated into intelligence mechanisms and thus establish cultural intelligence (CULTIN) … This type of intelligence concerns the ability to engage in a set of behaviors that use language, interpersonal skills and qualities appropriately tuned to the culture-based values and attitudes of interpersonal skills and qualities appropriately tuned to the culture-based values and attitudes of the people with whom one interacts … In the military sense, cultural intelligence is a complicated pursuit in

anthropology, psychology, communications, sociology, history and, above all, military doctrine.[9]

Additionally, the *Cultural Generic Information Requirements Handbook* for the Marines explained, "Cultural intelligence is the analysis and understanding of groups of people and the reasons they do the things they do." It clarified, "Cultural intelligence is not a list of 'do's and don'ts.' It is gaining an understanding of the mind set of local populations to support the commander's decision making and help drive operations."[10]

A further definition is provided by Commander, U.S. Navy, John P. Coles. He defined CQ as "analyzed social, political, economic, and other demographic information that provides understanding of a people or nation's history, institutions, psychology, beliefs (such as religion), and behaviors." He asserted, "It helps provide understanding as to why a people act as they do and what they think. Cultural intelligence provides a baseline for education and designing successful strategies to interact with foreign peoples whether they are allies, neutrals, people of an occupied territory, or enemy ... Cultural intelligence is more than demographics. It provides understanding of not only how other groups act but why."[11]

The French military definition of operational culture — or CQ in our terms — echoes these previous definitions: "Operational culture is the understanding of foreign cultural norms, beliefs and attitudes: it is an operationally relevant field guide used by general officers as well as infantry squad leaders to navigate a complex human terrain."[12]

Indeed, there exists a multitude of definitions that contain overlapping themes and ideas. Yet there still lacks a precise and clear definition of CQ that can be used as a practical starting point for teaching and learning how to apply enhanced levels of CQ when dealing with the contemporary operating environment.

This chapter builds on both the civilian literature about CQ and the military concerns and definitions of CQ in order to establish a clear understanding of what CQ is. It also returns to the earlier discussion on culture and situates the definition of CQ within the basic building blocks of culture (i.e., beliefs, values, attitudes, and behaviours). As we've by now deduced, CQ is the ability to recognize the shared beliefs, values, attitudes, and behaviours of a group of people and, most importantly, to apply this knowledge toward a particular goal.[13] More specifically, CQ refers to the cognitive, motivational, and behavioural capacities to understand and effectively respond to the beliefs, values, attitudes, and behaviours of individuals and institutions of their own and other groups, societies, and cultures under complex and changing circumstances in order to affect a desired end state.

CQ has four principle components (see Figure 3): first, one must clearly understand their own national objective and/or goal of applying enhanced CQ; second, individuals require region-specific knowledge and awareness; third, they need the ability, or skill set, and motivation to apply enhanced CQ; and finally, they need to exhibit the appropriate behaviour in order to achieve desired objectives.

CQ COMPONENTS

1. National objective and/or goal
2. Region specific knowledge/awareness
3. Ability (or skill set) and motivation
4. Appropriate behaviour

Figure 3. CQ components.

CQ must be applied in the context of the national, international, host nation, and enemy domains in order to be effective in the COE. Similar to a picture on a puzzle box, the "four CQ domain paradigm" provides the framework for where individual cultural knowledge pieces fit in the global context. Specific culture, country, or area cultural awareness provides details for each piece of the puzzle. Without both, the overarching conceptualization provided by the four CQ domain paradigm and the individual pieces established through country and even area specific cultural awareness, the puzzle cannot be put together.

The Four CQ Domain Paradigm

CQ empowers individuals to see "reality" through the eyes of another culture, specifically the one with which they are interacting. In turn, this ability provides individuals with some of the knowledge necessary for adapting their attitudes and behaviours to better influence the target audience in order to achieve specific aims. For the most part, the CF must simultaneously function in a multitude of cultural circumstances (see Figure 4). In order to be effective in all areas, members must demonstrate enhanced CQ specific to their target audience while also recognizing that their actions may be judged by any group of people. For instance, as Chapter Eight will underscore, behaviour

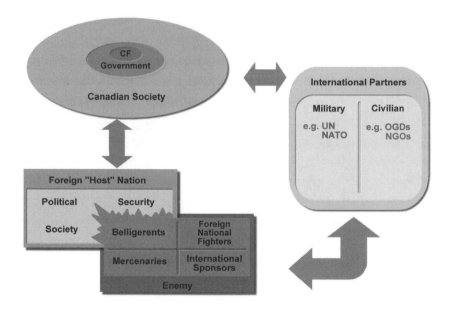

Figure 4. The four CQ domains: national, international, host nation, and enemy.

that may be acceptable to the host nation's culture may not be acceptable within Canadian culture and vice versa. With globalization and the proliferation of the media, actions in one domain can and likely will be judged by a variety of audiences. Therefore, behaviours must be acceptable across the four domains. Demonstrating enhanced CQ requires an appreciation of the role of the CF within the broader spectrum of Canadian society, the role the CF plays in multinational alliances, the complexities that may arise when operating in an overseas environment, particularly with host nation institutions and populations, as well as an in-depth understanding of the "enemy."

National Domain: Winning and Keeping the "Hearts and Minds" of Canadians

For CF members, understanding the beliefs, values, and customs that comprise Canadian culture is important because the CF both represents and serves that culture. After all, a military that serves a democratic nation cannot be fully successful if the will of the home population does not support a specific mission. As such, it is imperative that a military intimately understand its own societal attitudes and values so that it can maximize its support from its own citizenry. Only in this way can they be assured of the necessary support to achieve mission success, particularly for difficult, prolonged operations.

This is now more important than ever. The omnipresent twenty-first century media, with its ability to project an event around the globe "as it happens" exacerbates this point. As Colonel Fred Lewis, a former deputy commander of Task Force Afghanistan asserted, "The will of the Canadian people is our center of gravity. So, define center of gravity as our strength. If our strength fails, we lose."[14]

As Colonel Lewis argued, retaining public support for the mission is paramount to success. In order to retain public support for the mission, CF members must understand what Canadians value. An example that specifically indicates the Canadian public's desire to have their beliefs, values, and attitudes reflected in the behaviours of their soldiers, regardless of location, is the national media attention paid in the spring of 2007 to the alleged beatings of Afghan detainees who had been captured by Canadians and then released to Afghan authorities. Following their release, some detainees were allegedly beaten. The fact that Canadians handed over prisoners supposedly knowing that there was a great likelihood that they would be beaten by Afghan security forces caused some Canadians to question the morality of the mission.

Licia Corbella, a reporter with the *Toronto Sun* remarked on the irony of the situation. She observed that the fact that "the Afghan authorities beat prisoners is hardly surprising when one understands the [Afghan] culture a bit better." Given the uproar in Canada, however, she concluded, "Perhaps, thanks in part to Canada, [Afghan] prisons will be one of the first places in Afghanistan where beatings are not the norm."[15] Indeed, the reaction to the "detainee situation" suggests that many Canadians do not want to support a mission that does not continuously uphold Canadian beliefs, values, and attitudes, even in areas that clearly have different and opposing beliefs and values.[16] In fact, opinion polls and surveys demonstrate that support for the war effort diminishes as collateral damage, unethical conduct, and/or friendly force casualties are reported.[17]

Clearly, if a military that serves a democratic nation does not understand the culture of the society it serves, then it is doomed for failure. As former Harvard professor and Liberal Party leader Michael Ignatieff noted, "A military force in a democracy can only retain its legitimacy, its self-confidence, and its public support if it plays by the rules, if it refuses to fight dirty." However, he did acknowledge that "all of the wars and challenges that you face are coming at you from people who definitely and most emphatically fight dirty."[18] Indeed, Ignatieff's caution underlines the critical nature of understanding one's own societal values. It does not matter how the enemy conducts himself, to the Canadian people it matters how their soldiers behave and fight. Support for the cause can be lost both at home and in the country of operations if unethical behaviour or conduct contrary to international conventions occurs. In fact, American Lieutenant-General James N. Mattis warned American service personnel "not [to] create more enemies than you take out by some immoral act."[19]

Without a doubt, mission success hinges on maintaining the support of one's own society. Certainly, the mission needs to be judged as valuable by the society a military serves. Without an understanding of national culture, commanders and their soldiers can very quickly alienate their national support base and, thus, jeopardize the mission.

International Domain: Playing with Others —
Military Coalitions, Inter-Governmental Organizations,
Non-Governmental Organizations, and Host Nation Partners

Exhibiting enhanced CQ is increasingly important in the COE as greater emphasis is being placed on coalition operations. The COE has necessitated the creation of international coalitions of the willing to share the responsibility of ensuring global stability. Nations contribute members to military coalitions and intergovernmental and international organizations. In addition, individuals from a variety of national backgrounds join non-governmental organizations. All of these disparate groups operate in the same theatre and each has its own specific objectives, beliefs about the best course of action to take, and each has its own national and/or organizational culture.

To facilitate co-operation and effectiveness, with the ultimate goal of mission success, participants at all levels require enhanced CQ. While the array of groups and organizations that operate in unstable areas are usually working to achieve the same goals, (i.e., peace and stability), organizationally each group/organization will have its own unique responsibilities and tasks within a certain area. Moreover, they often operate under a variety of different agendas, assumptions, priorities, rules of engagements, national chains of command, and caveats.

Not surprisingly, unity of command — defined as the overall command of an area by one individual or organization — is rarely possible in complex situations involving multiple players.[20] In fact, unity of command is often not even present amongst different Canadian governmental departments.[21] However, unity of effort, meaning the co-operative alignment of agencies towards the same goal with minimal duplication of effort, can and should be achieved.

Enhanced CQ is paramount for achieving unity of effort in the COE. Beyond having different mandates and priorities, part of the problem is that some organizations are military, while others are civilian. The cultural divergence between the two is huge. For example, military organizations strive for uniformity, a clear plan, decisive decisions, speed of action, and acceptance of risk. Conversely, aid agencies and diplomats prefer a slower, long-term, more risk-averse, dialogue-intensive, and consensus-based approach. If one wishes to make progress in such a working environment these differences are important to recognize, acknowledge, and factor in when attempting to create a productive working environment, map out a plan of action, and execute a "campaign plan." In fact, one senior Army officer remarked of working with other Canadian governmental departments, "The greatest problem is one of ignorance. None of the players fully understand who the other participants are. Other government departments and civilian agencies are normally not accustomed to military directness or command structure."[22]

Exhibiting enhanced CQ in order to achieve unity of effort is particularly important as the CF is increasingly called on to operate within inter-governmental organizations (IGOs), such as the United Nations (UN) and the North Atlantic Treaty Organization (NATO), with other governmental departments (OGDs) from Canada, and domestic and international non-governmental organizations (NGOs). While some of these organizations are also Canadian, all have unique cultures. Understanding their beliefs, values, and attitudes, as well as appreciating how they see you, can lead to a more effective, not to mention harmonious, work relationship and dialogue between organizations, increasing the likelihood of mission success, usually in a shorter timeframe.

The benefits of enhanced CQ when dealing with other coalition military partners, IGOs, OGDs, and NGOs — particularly for achieving unity of effort — are important for a number of reasons. First, unity of effort minimizes redundant behaviour (i.e., duplication of effort within and between military contingents, national governments, or OGDs). Effective communication between groups helps to establish trust, credibility, and dialogue allowing for a "team" approach to problem solving rather than an "individual" approach. For example, when "Group A" says they are performing "X," CQ helps to predict the likelihood that the event will occur, the approach they will take, and the timeline. Armed with that knowledge you can determine if supplemental action is required and, if so, your best plan of action to complement that of the other partner or overall coalition. In essence, co-operation and an understanding of what is important to other allies or coalition partners, as well as their abilities to accomplish tasks, can provide the basis for effective sharing of tasks and responsibilities that lessens the load for all since redundancy and overlap is removed.

Second, unity of effort assures that pertinent and essential information is shared between organizations and that everyone is working towards the same long-term goal(s). It allows allies and coalition partners to be working on a level playing field and assures that pertinent information is shared with the right people. As such, a more complete picture or situational awareness is possible since, at least in theory, the best available information is available to those who need it.

Understanding the beliefs, values, attitudes, and behaviours of those you work with and acting in a complementary manner increases the overall effectiveness of the whole group. As such, CQ is an essential tool when dealing with allies, coalition partners, and other partners in the COE.

Host Nation Domain: Applying CQ in an Unfamiliar and Hostile Environment

When operating in a foreign environment, it is essential to understand the culture of the host nation (HN) population. A commander or any operator within an area of operation must have a clear understanding of who will oppose stabilization efforts and what motivates them to do so. They also need to know the best way to sway host nation inhabitants to their side. Adherence or, at minimum, respect for their culture and values is essential in winning the hearts and minds of locals. Yet one must also be conscious of one's own societal expectations. Unfortunately, as Carol McCann has pointed out, "Know your adversary has become a canon of war since time immemorial; understanding the broader [host nation] population was less customary and it has taken time for militaries to recognize that reality and adjust."[23]

Enhanced CQ offers one of the few possible solutions to this complex operating environment. Success in counter-insurgencies, specifically in locations such as Afghanistan, depends on winning the hearts and minds of the populace. As Lieutenant-Colonel Ian Hope asserted, "You cannot win without the trust of the local people."[24] And you cannot earn that trust if you do not understand them as a people and as a culture. Most military practitioners and strategists argue that the HN population is the centre of gravity for success in theatre (although an equally compelling case can be made for domestic support in regards to maintaining a respective national contingent in Afghanistan to prosecute the mission for example). The trust of the locals has to be earned through concrete action. Without an understanding of what is important and what behaviours will be seen as credible, their co-operation would be difficult to attain. What it boils down to is that building trust and credibility take time and are difficult tasks. Moreover, they are reliant on cultural intelligence. You need to appreciate the beliefs, values, and attitudes of the host nation population and act accordingly.

In order to gain the trust of local populations you need to appreciate how others see you — another dimension of the COE that CQ helps you attain. For example, an American veteran of Iraq acknowledged of his time there,

> I must do more than just train, advise and fight with my Iraqi friend. I must go out of my way every single day to disprove the 'Ugly American' label that is attached to me. I must approach every personal

> interaction as a singular opportunity to battle the insurgency and then realize that my interactions with each and every Iraqi do have lasting and very strategic consequences.[25]

Certainly, viewing yourself through the eyes of HN members while being cognizant of the environment, human and physical, will help you make good decisions when trying to influence HN peoples.

Building trust and credibility for your mission within the host nation population will build popular support for the HN national government. With increased popular support comes stability and security enhancements. For instance, the population will start to deny support to insurgents, consequently increasing its co-operation and direct support to the national government and coalition. This action will lead to increased security through information on insurgent movement and intent, and denying the same to the enemy. With enhanced security comes increased economic prosperity as people begin to believe that there is a prosperous future through alignment with the national government and coalition forces. This co-operation is symbiotic as security fuels reconstruction and development, and more reconstruction and development feed greater security.

In fact, it is exactly this type of CQ empowered behaviour that senior commanders are now overtly recommending for use in Afghanistan. General David McKiernan, commander, U.S. Forces Afghanistan/International Security Assistance Forces Afghanistan, admitted that "there is no purely military solution to the situation in Afghanistan … Ultimately, the solution must be a political one that is Afghan led." Acknowledging that perceptions are important, military members were reminded to "maintain the trust and respect of Afghans…. [To d]emonstrate respect and consideration for the Afghan people, their culture, customs, and religion … Avoid insults, inappropriate gestures, unnecessary brandishing of weapons, and aggressive driving that Afghans may perceive as offensive, threatening, or reckless."[26] Clearly, perceptions — whether justified or not — are important to the COE. In fact, McKiernan was overt in his directive: "Win the battle of perceptions."

He explained, "… inform and shape the perceptions, attitudes, understanding, and behaviour of key population groups. Consistently find ways to win the battle of perception." He also admitted, "Every insurgent action is designed to either influence the attitudes and perceptions of these population groups or to take advantage of local disenchantment to meet their own ends … In the competition for influence, we must be more agile and effective than the enemy."[27]

Complicating this process, as Figure 4 illustrates, is the fact that there are several different elements at play in the HN domain. HN populations can generally be divided into political, security, civilian, and belligerent elements. One of the goals of operations in the contemporary operating environment is to remove the belligerents from the HN while avoiding alienating the rest of the host nation population. Notably, as illustrated in the figure, belligerents can permeate the entire HN society including the political and security infrastructure. Enhanced CQ can help you identify friend from foe in a difficult environment. For example, understanding nuances in speech and gestures (helped by interpreters when necessary) can provide clues as to the presence of belligerents, which facilitates mobility and situational awareness on the ground.

Individuals with good CQ and cultural awareness of the area are able to gain a greater situational awareness of their environment. Armed with competent knowledgeable interpreters, they can also rely on more than just verbatim translations. In fact, they will be able to understand nuances that are missed by those with only a basic understanding of the language and culture. As such they will be privy to more meaningful messages. In fact, the message, through the means in which it is expressed (e.g., pauses, ambiguities, etc.), might have less to do with what is being said and more to do with how it is being said.

Being savvy of cultural cues can also help you determine if locals are "willingly" supporting insurgents. This can help you determine how to influence locals to your way of thinking. For example, in an area where insurgents are coercing locals to co-operate by threat of punishment, securing the area of operation and assuring the locals of your long-term commitment to them can help them side with you.

Enhanced CQ is essential for success in dealing with host nation populations in the COE. Not only does it aid in identifying friend from foe but, more importantly, it provides you with a useful tool for creating more of the former (and consequently less of the later) amongst host nation inhabitants.

Enemy Domain: Knowing the Enemy

Gaining a better understanding of one's adversaries is equally as empowering. Abandoning preconceived, superficial, or erroneous perceptions and actually endeavouring to fully comprehend the "enemy" can provide invaluable insights into their attitudes, behaviours, decision making, and motivations. This knowledge can provide options and strategies for disrupting, neutralizing and defeating adversaries by potentially addressing real or perceived grievances, discrediting their informational/ideological messages by eroding the support bases, disrupting their decision-making processes and alliances, and possibly co-opting the more moderate adversarial membership. The first task, however, as illustrated in Figure 4, is to fully understand who your enemy is. After all, your adversaries are not normally homogeneous. Within the myriad of antagonists each group can have disparate beliefs, motives, incentives, and rationales for fighting or opposing government authority and coalition forces. CQ is essential for understanding the enemy, whether as part of the information operation (IO) campaign to discredit a particular opponent with a specific target audience; the targeting campaign to understand how decisions are made and by whom; or by attacking alliances or support along tribal lines taking advantage of historic tensions and animosities.

Clearly, enhanced CQ is essential if a military force wishes to successfully defeat opposing forces, particularly in today's complex operating environment such as Afghanistan or Iraq. For example, a Canadian lieutenant commented of the ongoing fight with Taliban that not only are they a worthy opponent because they are fighting on their "home turf," but even more difficult to combat is the fact that "they have the belief that they're doing the right thing. You're combating that ideology, so you can't underestimate them."[28] Only by understanding the beliefs, values, attitudes, and behaviours (to name but a few factors) of the enemy can a military be successful. With this knowledge friendly forces can begin to target and dismantle the enemy's IO campaign, develop a targeting plan for kinetic strikes against enemy strongholds, and begin to erode the sympathetic HN support for the enemy and gain that of the host nation population for itself. Moreover, enhanced CQ can also assist in predicting likely enemy behaviour and thereby allow you to take the initiative.

"Know your enemy" is an age-old adage of war. What we should be asking now is how can we use this information to our advantage?

Demonstrating enhanced CQ in each domain is important for success in the COE. This does not mean that people should be cultural chameleons as they jump between each domain; rather, individuals need to balance the knowledge that they acquire of each domain and apply it in a manner that allows them to further their goals and to achieve the necessary and desired national objectives. For the CF, these goals should ultimately align with those of the Canadian government and population and, as Chapter Eight highlights, should be reflective of Canadian cultural values. While CQ is an important tool for all military members, as well as individuals from other governmental departments and agencies, it is of particular value for SOF. As such, the next chapter will focus specifically on the SOF/CQ interface.

PART III

Enabling the Force:
the SOF-CQ Interface

Chapter 6

The Application of CQ to SOF Missions

Cultural intelligence is a critical component of special operation forces operations. SOF operations are intelligence driven and often rooted in the very fibre of the communities in which they operate. As SOF face ethereal adversaries who utilize asymmetric methods to conduct conflict and war, and who are normally embedded within the societies they target to dismantle, an understanding of the beliefs, values, and attitudes that contribute to the decision making processes and behaviours, in short the cultures of those with whom SOF interact, is critical. In a struggle against an enemy who is capable of hiding behind the rights, freedoms, and protections of the societies that they seek to destroy, CQ offers an important tool that will increase the effectiveness of SOF by providing them with a better understanding of, and connection to, audiences that are key to SOF operations.

CQ should not be seen as merely a tool, rather it is a fundamental critical enabler of success in all SOF operations and activities. Its importance extends beyond operations and applies equally to networking and building relations within the Canadian Forces (i.e., among other services), other government departments, and equally with allies, coalition partners, and other international agencies.

The SOF/CQ Interface

The previous chapter outlined the importance of CQ to military operations in the larger context. This chapter will specifically focus on the importance of CQ within the SOF context, which is starkly evident when examined within the four paradigm model. The following analysis will provide a vivid image of the benefit of CQ to SOF activities and operations.

National Domain

Within the domestic realm there are a number of audiences that are critical for SOF to fully understand — each with its specific beliefs, values, and attitudes, and consequent behaviours. The first target domestic audience is the Canadian general public. Understanding Canadian beliefs, values, and attitudes is important for a number of reasons. First, public confidence and support is crucial to the continuing vitality of the Canadian Forces (CF) and Canadian Special Operations Forces (CANSOF). The "decade of darkness" in the 1990s, when a series of scandals eroded governmental and public confidence and support in the CF, demonstrated the danger of losing touch with Canadian societal sensitivities and beliefs in such basic concepts as accountability, integrity, and transparency.[1] This erosion in CF support impacted the Department of National Defence (DND) and the CF in a myriad of ways from budgetary support to recruiting and the ability to investigate and regulate itself as an autonomous profession. In essence, public support engenders political support, which leads to credibility and trust, which leads to freedom of action. Indeed, continuing Canadian participation in Afghanistan is directly tied to public sentiment and support.[2]

A "cultural" comprehension of the Canadian general public also has impacts on recruiting. An understanding of what is important to Canadians, what triggers their commitment and support, is key to developing the necessary approaches to attract young Canadians to join the CF and, specifically, the CANSOF community. It also assists in ensuring a support base exists if the CANSOF community is ever threatened or in crisis. If Canadians understand their CANSOF organizations and members, if there is deep-rooted connection between the public and CANSOF — particularly its mission and importance to national security — temporary crises or scandals will be less traumatic and have a less lasting effect. For instance, numerous scandals and challenges of British SAS practices in Northern Ireland and elsewhere rarely created a long-term problem for the elite regiment since it has always, at least in contemporary memory, been ensconced as an important national institution. This is a direct result of the historic and carefully crafted information campaign that successfully appealed to the British public and politicians. As such, an attack on the British SAS is in many ways an assault on British national security and military capability, which is unacceptable to most Britons and their politicians.

Finally, a cultural understanding of Canadians is an important source of information. As the threat to Western societies grows through the interconnected globalized world, through radicalization of homegrown terrorists on the Internet, or from domestic disenfranchised elements, SOF will increasingly be called on to assist law enforcement agencies (LEAs) in a domestic context. Understanding what's important to Canadians from a cultural, ideological, and/or attitudinal perspective will be critical for ensuring active support of SOF and to prevent alienation, passivity, or even active resistance while assisting LEAs in Canada.

Another key domestic audience for SOF, and one for which CQ is vital, is that of other government departments (OGDs). In the current complex security environment integrated operations — that is, security operations that require the co-operation of all military services (i.e., joint), as well as LEAs and other governmental departments, (e.g., Department of Foreign Affairs and International Trade (DFAIT), Public Safety, the Royal Canadian Mounted Police (RCMP), Public Health Canada, and Transport Canada) — will be on the increase. Personal relationships and trust will be key. However, since the military has a starkly different culture than the OGDs relations between the different entities have been a tale of mistrust, misunderstanding, alienation, and awkwardness. Much of this is due to a complete lack of understanding of the cultural make-up, decision making processes, and expectations of the various OGDs. For SOF to gain, nurture, and maintain the necessary relationships that engender co-operation, influence and trust will require a conscious effort to increase CQ with OGDs.

Success in this realm will have a direct impact on co-operative ventures, whether operations, policies, or the sharing of information, TTPs, or resources. Cultural understanding will remove suspicion and build credibility and trust, which, as noted, equates to freedom of action. It will promote co-operation and mutual assistance, which will in turn help dissipate bureaucratic inertia and build protocols and frameworks necessary for crisis decision making and co-operative action. It all starts with being able to see reality through the eyes of the other government departments and using that knowledge to help shape and influence the outcomes you require.

The final domestic audience for which CQ is fundamental to success is the internal CF audience. Often overlooked, the CF consists of several subcultures, the most obvious being the four distinct services (i.e., the navy, army, air force, and SOF). Without a deep and solid understanding of the CF overriding culture and the specific subcultures, CANSOF will be condemned to repeatedly fight the same tedious battles for resources (i.e., personnel, money, etc.). Understanding what drives competitors and/or potential allies is critical. Simply knowing the beliefs, values, attitudes, traditions, and decision making protocols — in short, what is important to the other services — will assist in eroding suspicion, animosity, and rivalry. More importantly, it will build the foundations for co-operation, resource sharing, and operational support. It will also assist in recruiting the necessary individuals from the other services as SOF is seen as a partner and sister service vice a competitor or rival.

International Domain

The international benefit of CQ for SOF, whether allies, coalition partners, government agencies, international organizations or agencies, or non-governmental organizations follows a similar rationale, as already noted. Quite simply, understanding those you work with makes for smoother relationships, better communication, and understanding and, therefore, more effective operations.

Allies and coalition partners, including our closest allies, the Americans and the British, have distinctly different cultures from ours. Moreover, our other European allies and coalition partners have cultures that vary even more from our own. It is critical to understand these differences and to know how and why they make decisions, what is important to them, and how to influence them if need be. Effective relationships, based on high levels of CQ, will assist in gaining support for operations, whether in the form of intelligence, enablers (e.g., ISR, fires), or troop commitment. It can also lead to co-operative ventures and access to sensitive equipment and/or technologies.

Effective CQ will also enhance communications and interaction by improving relations. High CQ will ensure that both parties actually communicate what is meant rather than what is perceived. Proper interpersonal skills (i.e., informal personal chat prior to getting to business), verbal expressions understood by both parties (i.e., avoiding jargon or slang known only to one party and that may have ambiguous or potentially negative meaning to another), and proper body language (i.e., that may be innocuous to one party but offensive to another) will enhance clarity and effectiveness of communications and ensure there is no confusion or breakdown due to misunderstanding. It will also build potentially lasting relationships.

Additionally, this level of understanding will assist in comprehending why partners act the way they do. That way a lot of frustration and criticism can be avoided, improving relations. It is important to understand that not all nations/armies operate as the Canadians do and, therefore, delays in decision making, approval processes, and expectations will differ. In order to impact those systems or organizations it is sometimes best to operate within their parameters as opposed to "butting heads" and building walls through an aggressive, myopic approach that is centred on an inward perspective of "reality."

This applies equally, if not more so, when dealing with international organizations and agencies (e.g., United Nations, World Food Program) or NGOs.[3] A strict military approach will alienate any individuals and organizations that already have a negative bias against the military in general and against secretive elite SOF organizations in particular. Understanding these biases and utilizing CQ to make these civilian partners feel at ease, open, and receptive to SOF advice and requests will pay huge dividends since these actors play an important role in the security environment of today and tomorrow, especially in counter-insurgency operations. These institutions represent the development and reconstruction pillars, as well as political governance and reform. Moreover, they have information and access to individuals and information that may not be as easily accessed, or accessed at all, by SOF operators. Therefore, they represent a potential, if not vital, pool of information. A failure to access and leverage these domains and work within an integrated manner will equate to operational failure. That undesirable end state can be avoided through the effective application of CQ.

CQ is also vital to the CANSOF task set of Defence, Diplomacy, and Military Assistance (DDMA).[4] Whenever training foreign or indigenous forces in counter-terrorism, internal defence, guerilla warfare, or any form of security operations, understanding your audience is fundamental. What resonates with them? What engages them? How do you get them to listen and fully participate? How do you develop bonds of trust and credibility? How do you appeal to their sense of duty and honour? How do you create lasting bonds of friendship and commitment?

In short, CQ is a vital force multiplier for SOF in its relations and operations with international forces, both military and civilian. The proper utilization and application of CQ will enhance comprehension of, and communications with, our partners, resulting in more effective outcomes. After all, CQ is a tool to assist with achieving a specified goal.

Host Nation Domain

The importance of CQ for SOF when dealing with host nation populations, political decision makers, and military or police agencies follows rationally from what has already been discussed.[5] For instance, host nation governmental officials or organizations represent another of our coalition partners. CQ is important when dealing with those entities too.

In today's security environment, particularly in the counter-insurgency context, "people are the prize." They represent the centre of gravity in the struggle for dominance between governmental authorities and the insurgents who wish to usurp them. Both groups are trying to win the hearts and minds of the populace. However, without a solid grasp of CQ it is impossible to establish credibility and trust in order to win over the population. Instead, a lack of CQ will work to alienate, insult, and marginalize the very people you wish to influence. At worst, a lack of CQ will drive the population to the enemy, at best win their neutrality or passivity. But even neutrality is a failure as it will not assist SOF or conventional forces in leveraging the population to help win the fight against the insurgents.

Understanding the culture — what is important to them, their value system, how they make decisions, what is acceptable behaviour in their eyes, respecting their traditions and behaving accordingly — will go a long way to earning their respect and trust. It will ensure SOF actions do more good than harm. In turn, generating the support of the populace, which has a direct effect on operations. The support and co-operation of the population will create a more effective operating environment for friendly forces and deny the same to the enemy. Globally, it can enhance force protection and reconstruction and development, while increasing information flow. Specifically, it can:

a. provide information on adversary movements, identities, and intentions;

b. warn of adversary weapons and explosive caches, safe houses, ambush locations, and IED placements;

c. provide information on "communities" and define who belongs and who does not; how authority and power are defined and codified; who are the power brokers; and how resources are managed;

d. provide information on key personalities, decision makers, and facilitators who can assist in mobilizing a target audience;

e. define rules for interaction;

f. explain relationships and social networks;

g. provide information on local/regional atmospherics with regard to culture, economics, demographics, and social issues;

h. provide information on topographical issues such as best routes, environmental/ground limitations, and restrictions;

i. enhance co-operation and participation in development, governance, and reconstruction initiatives;

j. generate support and participation for local security initiatives; and

k. increase overall support for national government and supporting coalition.

In sum, to win the support of the people, or in popular military jargon their "hearts and minds," it is critical to understand them. Specifically, it is essential that SOF operators can see through the eyes of the host nation populace and comprehend how their own words, behaviours, and actions are actually seen, interpreted, and understood by the host nation population. This requires detailed CQ.

Enemy Domain

The final domain is usually the area that intuitively receives the most attention, but often not in the correct context. Lieutenant-Colonel Adrian Bogart, a SOF officer with extensive experience in Afghanistan and Iraq observed, "We continually fail to understand our enemy." He elaborated, "We say that the enemy is not organized, yet he issues orders to his soldiers daily. We believe no command structure exists, yet the grand emirs, emirs and brigade commanders are in charge and directing their forces ... We believe the enemy is an undisciplined force, but he wears a standard uniform, has an area command that provides active security for the populace and is proud to be a Mujahideen."[6] Bogart's criticism is valid. Too often the enemy is analyzed, assessed, and rated based on our own cultural lens. Adversary strength, organization, hierarchy, TTPs, weapons, and equipment are rightfully important areas of concern. But so is the adversaries' beliefs, values, attitudes, motivational drivers, tribal affiliations, networks, and history; essentially, their culture.

To properly apply CQ to the enemy domain it is necessary to actually carefully define exactly who is "enemy" is. For example, the Taliban and al Qaeda are usually defined as the enemy/threat in Afghanistan and often they are used interchangeably. From a CQ perspective this is problematic. They are fundamentally different. From an attitudinal, ideological, motivational, and organizational perspective (just to mention a few) they are clearly dissimilar.

Similarly, such an unrefined outlook on the enemy/threat also limits the benefit that can be derived from CQ analysis. For instance, using the example of Afghanistan again, it must be noted that threats also emanate from criminal organizations, narco-traffickers, warlords, regional state rivals, and proxy forces supported by third party state actors with geo-political goals and aims.[7] From a CQ perspective, each of these actors presents a potentially diverse profile. As such, it is critical to understand the exact audience in each and every domain.

With respect to the "enemy" domain, applying CQ presents a valuable return on investment. Specifically, it can:

a. provide insight into enemy motivation that could allow for diffusion of grievances or the co-opting of moderates;

b. assist with debunking enemy information operations, propaganda, and recruiting messages by highlighting discrepancies, contradictions, and falsehoods;

c. provide understanding of decision making processes and value systems, thus furnishing possible weaknesses or stress points that can be manipulated;

d. assist with the understanding of a pattern of behaviour that can provide insight into targeting (both the enemy's and your own), attack preferences (i.e., timing, locations, type, targets), likely reactions given situational circumstances (e.g., if faced with military or police actions), and normal pattern of life;

e. assist with understanding history and symbology, which in turn provides insight into possible "safe areas" (sanctuary), historical, and/or preferred attack positions/zones, targets, and dates (i.e., historically, religiously, or ideologically significant);

f. provide insight into historic alliances and sponsors, which can lead to illuminating financing, supply nodes and routes, leadership engagements, and possible sanctuaries; and

g. provide insight into social networks, which provide information on targeting of key personalities (i.e., leaders, facilitators, specialists) and intelligence gathering activities.

The list is not meant to be definitive. Rather, it is meant to highlight the types of information that can be obtained from applying CQ when analyzing the enemy domain. A genuine understanding of the enemy as they see themselves — beyond our interpretation of their culture — will yield the greatest benefit in the struggle to vanquish our adversaries.

CQ and the four paradigm model are not a "silver bullet" that will magically tame the ambiguous, chaotic, and volatile contemporary operating environment. However, it will assist and empower SOF operators, as well as any military or para-military force, or any other entity operating in the security environment, make better sense of the environment in which they operate, and increase their ability to influence and shape the attitudes of important target audiences. In this way, enhanced CQ is an excellent tool to help SOF achieve their aims. It is worth the time and other resources to develop these skills in SOF personnel.

Chapter 7

Developing CQ in SOF

There is no doubt that cultural intelligence (CQ) is a critical enabler in the contemporary operating environment (COE). Moreover, this connection is particularly true in the case of special operations forces (SOF). Just as one cannot effectively mass produce SOF operators rapidly following an emergency, one cannot quickly instill CQ in SOF following a deployment to an unfamiliar region and expect a successful outcome. As such, CQ needs to be thoroughly and consistently integrated into education, training, planning, and operations. It is not simply enough to recognize the problem. Echoing age-old truisms about insurgency and counter-insurgency warfare, in 2004 retired American Major-General Robert H. Scales commented, "This new era of war requires soldiers equipped with exceptional cultural awareness and an intuitive sense for the nature and character of war."[1]

Despite this, little has been done to correct the problem. No effort is spared to ensure soldiers are well-trained on weapon systems and vehicles, and tactics, techniques, and procedures (TTPs) for the tactical battle. Yet there does not appear to be any focus on ensuring soldiers and leaders understand the cultural and societal surroundings and context. As U.S. Lieutenant-General Thomas Metz argued in 2006, the enemy "is effectively using the global media to impede our operations by creating the perception that our combat operations are indiscriminate, disproportionate and in violation of the rules of war.... The truth of the matter is ... our enemy is better at integrating information-based operations, primarily through mass media, into his own operations than we are."[2] In fact, by and large

Western militaries are still failing in this regard or lagging behind the enemy. In 2009, U.S. Marine Corps Major Ben Connable noted, "Initial operations in Afghanistan and Iraq revealed three interrelated shortcomings in military cultural competency." He explained, "First, cultural training for troops, staffs, and commanders was utterly deficient. Second, military intelligence personnel were not prepared to read or analyze cultural terrain and lacked comprehensive data to constantly provide cultural analysis. Third, many staffs were incapable of using cultural terrain to their advantage, which resulted in an early series of wasted opportunities that fed the insurgencies and terrorist operations of the Taliban, Ba'athist insurgents and Al-Qaeda."[3] We need to reverse this trend. Western militaries need to take the initiative to maximize the cultural intelligence education and training that military members receive

As underscored throughout this book, people are the prize in the contemporary operating environment. Victory will be afforded to the side that is most adept at influencing public opinion and generating popular support. Consequently, behaving in a manner that demonstrates enhanced levels of CQ is not simply the moral, "politically correct" path to take. It is the most direct route to victory. In fact, in a recent report the commander of the North Atlantic Treaty Organization's International Security Assistance Force (ISAF), General Stanley McChrystal, was adamant in that regard. He stated, "We must fight the insurgents, and will use the tools at our disposal to both defeat the enemy and protect our forces. But we will not win based on the number of Taliban we kill, but instead on our ability to separate insurgents from the center of gravity — the people." He explained, "That means we must respect and protect the population from coercion and violence — and operate in a manner that will win their support ... This is different from conventional combat, and how we operate will determine the outcomes more than traditional measures, like capture of terrain or attrition of enemy forces." He cautioned, "We must avoid the trap of winning tactical victories — but suffering strategic defeats — by causing civilian casualties or excessive damages thus alienating the people."[4]

McChrystal's comments underscore the critical importance of CQ in the COE. Properly educated and trained soldiers and officers are the key to victory in the COE. This association is particularly true with regard to cultural intelligence. For today's soldier, who is usually called upon to act simultaneously as a warrior and a diplomat, there is no substitute for both education and training in order to perform effectively in the complex, ambiguous, volatile, and dynamic COE. As retired U.S. Army Colonel Gregory Fontenot explained, "Ambiguous, non-traditional adversaries seek new means to destroy, disrupt, or just outwait us.... Every day our adversaries rapidly adapt, requiring us to reassess how they think about themselves, their environment and us."[5] Fontenot's observation underscores the fact that we must do exactly the same thing.

Clearly, this type of operating environment demands a fluid, non-templated set of responses that can only come from a combination of education and training. Aided by the ever present media, the tactical decisions of any soldier can have far-reaching ramifications all the way up to the strategic level. Consequently, irrespective of rank or occupation, all soldiers need to be adept at CQ. As Lieutenant-Colonel John Conrad, a Canadian combat logistics officer observed, in the contemporary operating environment "all soldiers, regardless of rank, stature or cap badge, have to be prepared to fight ... there are no such words as *front* and *rear* anymore."[6] While Conrad was speaking about combat, his conclusions are equally (if not more) valid in the realm of culture and diplomacy. Indeed, addressing the importance of CQ, McChrystal warned the West, "The Taliban cannot militarily defeat us — but we can defeat ourselves."[7]

In the contemporary operating environment, where people are the prize, CQ is a crucial tool to have in your arsenal. Having already elaborated on its importance to the COE, it is important to determine how best to integrate education and training programs into the already full curriculum of military members.

What Should Be Taught

Prior to delving into what should be taught, it is important to distinguish education from training. As Ron Haycock, professor at the Royal Military College of Canada explained, training is "a predictable response to a predictable situation." On the other hand, education is "the reasoned response to an unpredictable situation — critical thinking in the face of the unknown."[8]

Haycock's colleague, Major David Last, elaborated on the concept, explaining that education "is the shaping of the mind." For professional officers, "There is no purpose without understanding. The officer's understanding must match that of society — otherwise he or she cannot serve it."[9]

John Cowan, former principal of the Royal Military College of Canada, elaborated on that point. He described how, "Today, when a young officer may be called upon to be a skilled leader, a technical expert, a diplomat, a warrior, and even an interpreter and an aid expert all at once there is no question that good training is not enough. Skills are not enough ... The job calls for judgement, that odd distillate of education, the thing which is left when the memorized facts have either fled or been smoothed into a point of view, the thing that cannot be taught directly, but which must be learned. Without the mature judgement which flows from education, we fall back on reflexes, which are damned fine things for handling known challenges, but which are manifestly unreliable when faced with new ones."[10]

There are benefits to both education and training for military members. Colonel Bernd Horn, also affiliated with the Royal Military College of Canada, is clear in his explanation of the benefits of a "soldier/scholar." He surmised, "A greater breadth of knowledge, tolerance to alternate interpretations and ideas, familiarity with critical debate and discussion, the honing of analytical skills, as well as the exposure to complete new bodies of literature and thought expand the mind and make the soldier that much more capable.... For far too long these two entities have remained apart when in fact they should be fused to strengthen both disciplines."[11]

However, that is not to say that training is not also vitally important to today's combatant. The beneficial effect of realistic training is timeless and undisputed. Research and studies have shown that "the general level of anxiety in combat would tend to be reduced insofar as the men derived from training a high degree of self-confidence about their ability to take care of themselves ... troops who expressed a high degree of self-confidence before combat were more likely to perform with relatively little fear during battle."[12] In fact, General William Slim of Burma fame in the Second World War, asserted, "Training was central to the discipline soldiers needed to control their fear, and that of their subordinates in battle; to allow them to think clearly and shoot straight in a crisis, and to inspire them to maximum physical and mental endeavour."[13]

In the end, it is a combination of both education and training, particularly in the realm of cultural intelligence, that will enable soldiers to be effective in the contemporary operating environment.

Education

In order to effectively respond to the often unpredictable situations faced by military members in the contemporary operating environment, officers and soldiers need to be able to critically assess the situation and determine the best course of action in a limited amount of time, often under direct stress, including life threatening situations. More often than not these critical situations will involve some type of cultural nuance. In basic terms, in addition to properly performing TTPs, conflict resolution in the COE will involve bridging cultural chasms in order to obtain a desired end state. As such, officers and soldiers need to learn how best to use the information at hand to afford the most desired results when dealing in intercultural situations. Essentially, they need to know how to demonstrate high CQ.

In order to demonstrate high CQ, individuals must be capable of critical thinking, understanding basic human behaviour and the concept of rationality, appreciating the basics of cultural groupings, as well as understanding and appreciating the role that perspective plays in people's configuration of the world, their place in it, and their view of your place in it. Learning these four foundational skill sets will enable soldiers to apply specific regional/cultural information about a particular group of people in order to further their cause and achieve their aim.

Critical thinking is perhaps the most important lesson to be learned as it enables the development of the other aforementioned skill sets. In short, "Critical thinking is that mode of thinking — about any subject, content, or problem — in which the thinker improves the quality of his or her thinking by skillfully [*sic*] taking charge of the structures inherent in thinking and imposing intellectual standards upon them." In essence, "Critical thinking is the intellectually disciplined process of actively and skillfully [*sic*] conceptualizing, applying, analyzing, synthesizing, and/or evaluating information gathered from, or generated by, observation, experience, reflection, reasoning, or communication, as a guide to belief and action."[14]

Critical thinking is not something that is trainable and despite the plethora of college and university courses called "Critical Thinking," it is not really a teachable subject.[15] It is also not a skill that one either has or does not have. Rather, it is a skill that is present by degree. While it cannot be overtly taught, paradoxically it is a skill that can be learned through experience, increased knowledge, and continuously questioning "facts." Part of critical thinking is asking why some things are fundamentally held beliefs. By doing so one can gain insight into why we believe certain things and what the "truth" really is.[16] In short, critical thinking is "self-directed, self-disciplined, self-monitored, and self-corrective thinking."[17] It is a skill that is developed over time through increased awareness of self and the surrounding environment.

Critical thinking enables individuals to:

1. ask pertinent questions and identify relevant problems;
2. gather and assess relevant information;
3. think with an open mind and, thereby, question assumptions;

4. communicate effectively with others in finding solutions to complex problems (both in terms of delivering and receiving information); and

5. come to well-reasoned conclusions and solutions while accurately predicting consequences of action/inaction.[18]

Examining cultural constructs using critical thinking requires that individuals question their belief and value pairings in order to assess and, when necessary, realign attitudes and associated behaviours. It demands that people realize that cultures are socially constructed ideas about the world. While some of these ideas may be based on "fact," others may be erroneous. Additionally, as explained in Chapter Four, values directly influence attitudes and behaviours that are based on specific beliefs. Critical thinking enables individuals to question these general assumptions about their own culture as well as other cultures and to break down some of the belief-value pairings.

If every person was a critical thinker at all times then the likely result would be a constant state of rationality. Of course this is not the case and people do not behave rationally at all times. Rather, as mentioned, critical thinking is applied by degree.[19] For example, someone may think critically about one aspect of their life but not question another. Nonetheless, basic human nature dictates that people behave rationally most of the time. But without applying critical thinking to each situation "rational behaviour" becomes subjective.

In the disciplines of economics, sociology, and political science, rational decisions are those that are deemed optimal to produce the desired results. Thus, rational behaviour is the behaviour that most directly achieves a desired end state with the least amount of collateral damage (where collateral damage may negate the overall goal). In modern thought, the concept of rationality has often been associated with maximizing economic wealth while minimizing costs — a very utilitarian view of rationality. More recent scholarship challenges this assumption.[20]

This challenge is particularly pertinent when exploring cross-cultural relationships. While one can generally assume that behaviour that is largely free of emotional influence is aimed at achieving a desired outcome in the most cost-efficient way, this assumption does not mean that 1) all behaviour is planned and/or rational or free of emotion; or 2) that all desired outcomes are associated with economic profit. Thus, critically thinking about the problem from an alternate perspective can provide insight into how others, especially those from a different culture who hold different beliefs, values, and attitudes from your own, might act in a given situation. This task involves letting go of one's own preconceptions in order to see the world through someone else's eyes. As mentioned in Chapter Four, a behaviour that may seem rational and sane to one person may not seem rational to someone else. Regardless, understanding the concept of rational choice (i.e., making decisions that maximize profit and minimize loss) does not mean that you have to agree with the other person's choices or that you should judge them by ethical and/or moral standards. It simply means that you can learn to predict desired outcomes in others and which behaviours will most likely lead to those sets of conditions. Therefore, having a basic understanding of human behaviour and, in particular, how it applies to rational choice, makes it easier to predict the behaviour of others. Carol McCann, head of Defence Research Development Canada (DRDC)'s adversarial intent section, explains, "Preparing people to understand human behavior well ... would be a way to prepare the soldier well for a more human-oriented kind of conflict."[21] Moreover, appreciating the basic building blocks of culture will help facilitate this ability at a group level, especially when dealing with cross-cultural situations.

Understanding the basics of how cultures develop and are sustained is also important for effective cross-cultural communications because it enables you to think critically about culture and to appreciate and predict rational behaviour in groups where individuals are part of different cultures. One way to achieve this is to view culture through a lens that reflects belief — value parings with regard to broad social structures. As Chapter Four detailed, one way of making sense of this cultural quagmire is by applying

Geert Hofstede's four value dimensions: power distance, uncertainty avoidance, individualism-collectivism; and masculinity-femininity.[22] Certainly, other value dimensions can be applicable. What is important is to try to understand the society that you are dealing with in terms of broad strokes first and then to add in the detail afterward. As James A. Bates, the Unconventional Warfare Studies coordinator with the U.S. Joint Special Operations University at Hurlburt Field, Florida commented, "The answer [to conflict in the COE] lies in looking at the social system that supports and sustains the insurgents, then devising and executing a sustained engagement strategy that addresses and attacks every part of that system in an appropriate fashion."[23]

These broad social strokes should address "the social, ethnographic, cultural, economic, and political elements of the people among whom a force is operating."[24] As French Colonel (retired) Henri Bore explains, "The French military's operational culture syllabus examines foreign societies' cultural habits, traditional customs, social and political constructs, moral ideas, codes of honor, and ways of thinking ... Such knowledge helps commanders quickly identify and take advantage of psychological points of weakness and strength of the insurgent they are — or will be — fighting, as well as the local force they are — or will be — training. Furthermore, understanding what drives local authority and identifying who is really in charge helps commanders establish and enforce lines of communication with local political, religious, and military leaders...."[25] Additionally, this type of framework can also help you evaluate — and think critically about — your own society and will help you to appreciate how others see you.

When navigating the complex, ambiguous, volatile, dynamic, and dangerous geography that characterises the contemporary operating environment, an understanding of human behaviour at an individual and group level during periods of conflict is an unquestionable asset. As U.S. General (retired) Robert Scales remarked, "Every military leader, particularly those whose job is to practice war, must be given every opportunity to study war.... Every soldier regardless of grade or specialty should be given unfettered and continuous access to the best and most inclusive programs of war studies."[26]

Critically thinking about cultural constructs using models, such as Geert Hofstede's four value dimensions, and applying the concept of rational thought to predicting the behaviour of opponents leads directly into the fourth skill set that needs to be developed in order to effectively apply CQ to the COE: perspective. Appreciating and understanding the importance of perspective from an individual and cultural point of view is paramount to effectively applying CQ. As U.S. Major-General Benjamin C. Freakley, commanding general, CJTF-76, in Afghanistan in 2006, remarked,

> Cultural awareness will not necessarily always enable us to predict what the enemy and non-combatants will do, but it will help us better understand what motivates them, what is important to the host nation in which we serve, and how we can either elicit the support of the population or at least diminish their support and aid to the enemy.[27]

Fortunately, or unfortunately depending on your side of the argument, we are all limited by our own world views (perspective), which can lead to ethnocentrism. One of the major prerequisites for enhanced CQ is the ability to see the world from a different perspective, to see through the eyes of the "other" and thereby see how others see you. To apply this skill without moral or ethical judgement can help to mitigate ethnocentrism and errors in judgement that can be associated with a sentiment of cultural superiority. Thus, appreciating perspective is key to effectively applying CQ because it provides a fuller picture of the world and helps you safely navigate cultural minefields by understanding and predicting the behaviours of others.

While superficially the concepts of critical thinking, human behaviour, rationality, basic cultural structures, and perspective may seem simple and easy to learn, they are not. But they all become easier to apply with knowledge and time. The more one learns to question "truths," the more one will naturally default to critical thinking. However, you cannot be trained to simply ask why. Only through accumulation of knowledge and wisdom can you learn to reason why you think a certain way and to accept and challenge concepts concerning your environment. Critical thinking will also help with understanding human behaviour at the individual and group levels, as well as appreciating the role that perspective plays in our configuration of the world. As such, each of these skill sets needs to be developed. First, an appreciation of each one is required, then, through time and education, they should be continuously developed in the individual. As Scales so aptly commented, "Learning must be a life-long process."[28] Bore echoed these remarks stating that, "The primary lesson learned is that operational cultural understanding is a long-term process."[29] Appreciating these "basics" will facilitate the application of certain "trainable" qualities.

Training

When dealing with the ambiguities that arise within and across cultures it is nearly impossible to train for a specific set of responses that can be effectively applied to any situation. Nonetheless, there are some specifics about cross-cultural encounters as applied to the COE that can be trained for. Specifically, each member should be able to:

1. identify the requirements of the mission and recognize the tools at their disposal of which CQ should be central;
2. identify major aspects about the foreign culture that align with Geert Hofstede's four value dimensions (or another similar model);
3. develop basic communication skills for that area/region (recognize and appreciate differences in meaning in gestures and

125

non-verbal communication. For example, in some African countries the thumbs-up sign, which means everything is okay by Western standards, is considered a rude gesture); and

4. acquire basic language skills for that area/region.

While each of these requirements may be mission/region specific, providing a set of "facts" about the engagement, when applied with the four previously mentioned skill sets, will nonetheless provide the ammunition to effectively use CQ in the COE.

Soldiers can be trained in these four areas, where "predictable responses to predictable situations" are likely to occur. Without questioning or needing to think critically about the matter, soldiers should be able to perform all four of those tasks. They should know the answers by rote, just as they know the mechanics of their weapon. This information can be disseminated as fact and memorized to be readily applied as needed in the COE. Like learning how to use a firearm the training focuses primarily on enabling the individual to manipulate the weapon under a variety of circumstances, especially under severe stress. But this is not enough. The weapon's discharge, or for the sake of this discussion the CQ, must be correctly applied to the COE. For this to occur, training needs to be paired with education. A soldier can be trained in how to manipulate a weapon but s/he needs to be taught about its proper application, rules of engagement, and how to decide what is the best course of action. Like a rifle, CQ is a tool at the disposal of the soldier and requires training and education to be properly employed.

American Lieutenant-Colonel Prisco R. Hernandez, director for Reserve Component Programs, Army National Guard, at the Center for Army Tactics in Fort Leavenworth, Kansas, argued that the U.S. military needs to train its members in "cultural understanding," the grey area that exists between cultural awareness and cultural expertise. He elaborated, explaining that "The intent [of such training] is not to make the Soldier a regional or cultural expert. Such expertise requires many years of sustained study and immersion in a culture." Yet, he argued, soldiers need to be equipped with "skills to operate with true understanding — not simply awareness. This understanding would come from study in three distinct, but related, cognitive areas: history and culture, language, and practical application."[30] In essence: know the mission, know the cultural nuances, and be able to communicate effectively — including having a grasp of the host nation language — and know when and how to employ this knowledge.

In fact, there is little argument that this kind of training is essential for success in the COE. Scholars, analysts, commanders, and tactical practitioners all agree on the requirement. There is also general consensus that the more training and education an individual receives, the better it is for the individual and for mission success. The major stumbling block in allowing individuals to reach a complete level of expertise in all areas is the allocation of scarce resources, particularly time. This training, while continuous, must occur pre-deployment.

Unfortunately, this sequencing of required training is something that Western militaries tend to neglect: cultural training should precede the mission rather than lag behind deployments. On the job training, particularly when the operation includes combat, is far from ideal. For example, commenting on the U.S. Marines in the war in Iraq, Director of the Center for Research on Military Organizations David Segal,noted, "Three years into this war, they're figuring out how to fight it."[31]

This deficit was not always the case, and we should take a lesson from our past experiences. Retired U.S. air commando and rescue pilot, Richard D. Newton, who now serves as a faculty member of the Joint Special Operations University and as an adjunct faculty member at the U.S. Army School of Advanced Military Studies explains, "Special Forces training included a healthy dose of regional familiarity, local languages, cultural acumen, and instructor development ... A Special Forces soldier had to become part anthropologist, part diplomat, part organizational developer, and part cultural attaché as well as being an excellent soldier and trainer."[32] Clearly, these skills and knowledge were acquired prior to engagements. Speaking in more general spatial and temporal terms, cultural anthropologist

Montgomery McFate underscores the point that there was a time when "anthropologists excelled at bridging the gap between the military and tribes." She suggests in this regard that militaries return "back to the future."[33]

To summarize, training, in contrast to education, should be mission specific. It should clarify the requirements of the mission and enable soldiers to identify major aspects of the foreign culture and communicate effectively verbally as well as non-verbally. And it must happen prior to deployment into theatre. There is no dispute that more training is better than less — it is simply a case of allocating resources. However, until commanders recognize CQ for the vital enabler it is to mission success, scarce time will not likely be dedicated to disciplines that are still often seen as intangible "nice to haves." But, with the growing recognition of the importance of CQ to the COE, resources must be reallocated in acknowledgement of CQ as a central enabler and force multiplier.

Training should not negate the importance of education. Rather, the two should go hand in hand. Education should provide the greater context for how best to utilize specific knowledge about a region garnered through training. The question is what is the best way to disseminate both training and education to a group of people whose time is already at a premium and who are continuously engaged in the complex, ambiguous, volatile, dynamic, and dangerous COE?

How Curriculum Should Be Developed and Disseminated

There is no question that in order to operate effectively in the COE both cultural education and training are necessary. Several recommendations can be made for how to best go about this pursuit:

1. the "so what" factor of the importance of CQ to the COE should be continuously underscored by commanders, subject matter experts and intelligence analysts;[34]

2. education should be encouraged, facilitated and rewarded throughout members' careers;[35]
3. specific reading lists should be developed and material should be readably accessible, preferably online;
4. language training should be readily available;[36]
5. subject matter experts should be retained, help to identify what material needs to be available, and update reading lists and other teaching tools;[37]
6. discussion groups, led by subject matter experts (which can include academics, veterans, and foreign nationals, to name a few) should be readily available;
7. professional development sessions should regularly have a CQ component;
8. relevant personal experience should be shared and built upon, including the experiences of SOF operators, members of other governmental departments, non-governmental organizations, other professionals, and expatriates living in targeted countries;
9. real life scenarios should be recreated with role playing, particularly "Red-Teaming,"[38] and feedback from subject matter experts should be provided on the spot; and
10. time must be allocated for these activities by commanders to underscore the importance of the activities.

Leadership Responsibilities

What it all boils down to is that leaders must allocate the necessary time and resources to properly educate and train subordinates in areas related to the ability to demonstrate enhanced cultural intelligence. Leaders must recognize the importance of CQ to the COE and its importance as a force enabler and multiplier. Then they must convey that importance to their subordinates. As retired French Colonel Henri Bore remarked, "Ultimately, the battalion commander's operational culture training is driven by the idea that teaching leaders and soldiers how to think and operate in a foreign environment matters more than just teaching them what to think about it."[39] By inculcating the importance and benefit of understanding the attitudes, beliefs, values, and behavioural idiosyncrasies of other cultures, as well as your own society's and organization's culture and subcultures, leaders can better prepare and arm their subordinates for success in the COE.

They must also ensure that the appropriate resources are allocated to the educational effort. Words are not enough. They must underscore their commitment with action. They must clearly demonstrate that CQ training and education is important to them. They must clearly dispel the notion that it is merely "nice to have" or a discretionary activity. The clearest way to achieve that is to dedicate the necessary resources and personal attention to education and training. Leading by example is key. Leaders must undertake the education and training themselves and continually underscore its importance by providing examples and showcasing successful results directly attributed to proper use of CQ. Certainly, their personal conduct and example must always demonstrate advanced CQ. As such, leaders have a tremendous responsibility to instil CQ amongst their subordinates; to neglect to do so is akin to knowingly sending a soldier off to battle without the necessary equipment to get the job done. Many would argue that this would be unconscionable.

PART IV

Doing the "Right" Thing

Chapter 8

Ethical Considerations
of Employing CQ

The ethics of war are an extremely difficult subject. It is unlikely that there will ever be consensus as to the exact meaning of a "just war."[1] The very essence of war is to get your opponent to submit to your will. As Professor Robert G. Spulak Jr. records, "The enduring nature of war is that, within the strategic arena of conflict, we and our enemy are both striving to be able to destroy the other."[2] As such, each side feels that they are "justified" in their behaviour. While justification does not necessarily mean that actions are performed in an ethical manner, often the two are correlated. As social constructs each one acts independently of the other, although they work best when aligned, even if only in the minds of a few people. For example, it is easier to try to justify genocide on the basis of committing an ethical act for the benefit of a select group of people, such as the maintenance of the purity of a race, rather than for political/economic reasons. Although there is clearly no defence for such actions, those who choose to undertake such heinous acts often use ethics to justify their circumstances. Just as President George W. Bush so infamously polarized the world in terms of "Good versus Evil," others attempt to create clear dichotomies of right and wrong, ethical and unethical, where a continuum of grey exists.

The ethics of applying enhanced cultural intelligence as a tool in the contemporary operating environment is an equally challenging topic. After all, CQ is about manipulating people. While there is no formula that will provide an answer to all ethical questions, there are certain guidelines that should be followed. First, one needs to understand what ethics are, what ethical dilemmas are, and what factors should be taken into consideration when solving ethical dilemmas. Military members need to understand their responsibilities and obligations to the country and the society they serve and how best to resolve the mission in an ethical manner. When used correctly, CQ can help to facilitate ethical resolutions to conflict in the COE. While this chapter does not offer a prescript for how to behave ethically in all situations, it outlines the major questions that should be considered when faced with an ethical dilemma.

Defining Ethics

Ethics are a social construct. They have no meaning unto themselves, they are meaningful because people agree to their meaning with regard to moral behaviour.[3] As such, the meaning can easily change from one group of people to another and with time. As researcher Brooks Peterson remarked, "One person's perception of good, fair … may be seen by another person as completely unfair or even corrupt … cultural context determines what is right and what is wrong."[4]

One of the most common social constructs, and an easier one to conceptualize, is money. A U.S. one-hundred dollar bill on its own cannot keep you warm, feed you, or clothe you. However, it can be exchanged for goods that may fulfill those needs. The amount of merchandise that you can get for the money depends on a variety of things and is subject to fluctuation based on supply and demand. Although worthless on its own, the concept of money — cash, credit, or debit — continues to exist because people agree that it should. Ethics, while less concrete, operate in the same manner. Their meaning is only as strong as the value that people place on them.

According to the *Oxford Dictionary of Philosophy*, ethics is "the study of the concepts involved in practical reasoning: good, right, duty, obligation, virtue, freedom, rationality, choice."[5] On one hand, the study of ethics can "concern itself with a psychological or sociological analysis and explanation of our ethical judgments, showing what our approvals and disapprovals consist in and why we approve or disapprove what we do." On the other hand, "it may concern itself with establishing or recommending certain courses of action, ends, or ways of life as to be taken or pursued, either as right or as good or as virtuous or as wise, as over against others which are wrong, bad, vicious, or foolish."[6] The former seeks to understand why we think some things are good or bad, ethical or unethical, while the later prescribes an ethical way to live.

Ethical Dilemmas and Considerations

A dilemma is "a situation requiring a choice between equally undesirable alternatives."[7] The important factors of this definition are that 1) a decision has to be made (even if it is to choose not to do anything) and 2) neither option is desirable. The point is that you have to decide which course of action is the least negative.

An ethical dilemma involves the choice between two equally undesirable alternatives that will usually involve an apparent conflict between moral imperatives in which to obey one would transgress the other (i.e., competing values). A moral imperative is a principle originating inside a person's mind — based on their beliefs and values — that compels that person to act. For example, a moral imperative could include the belief that killing another human being is wrong in any situation. As such, the person would be against killing even as self-defence. However, if the same person also believed that life should be defended at all cost, then s/he would be facing an ethical dilemma if the only option was to kill or be killed. In this situation, the person would be faced with a conflict between two moral imperatives. To resolve the dilemma s/he would have to either kill their opponent or not defend themselves, neither option being ideal.

Beyond competing values, ethical dilemmas are further complicated by uncertainty. In many instances, the outcome of one's actions is not clear at the outset, which can complicate deciding which course of action is best or, in the case of an ethical dilemma, the least harmful. For instance, if a known dangerous assailant, terrorist, or insurgent leader escapes into a crowd of people and you are able to take the target out but you may also inflict collateral damage (i.e., kill one or more innocent civilians), is it ethical to proceed with the shot or airstrike? Does knowing the target is on their way to commit a heinous crime alter your decision? Certainly, uncertainty as to the outcome of your action or inaction can complicate an ethical dilemma.[8]

Many factors are taken into account, consciously and subconsciously, when resolving an ethical dilemma. First, personal ideas of what is right and wrong (ethical or unethical) come in to play, generally at the subconscious level, and are often rooted in cultural beliefs, values, and attitudes. Second, information and knowledge about the probability of an outcome will affect decisions. For instance, if you believe that you are 90 percent likely to be successful at shooting/ striking a single target in a crowd of innocent people, then your decision may be different than if you only thought you had a 10 percent chance of success.

Beyond immediate outcomes, potential long-term outcomes should also be considered and will factor into your decision. A classic example of this type of scenario is that of an overloaded lifeboat. If one person is not removed, the boat will sink, forcing the group to nominate a sacrificial lamb or face the consequence of sinking, putting all lives at risk. In cases like this many would reason that the "best" course of action is that which brings the greatest benefit to the greatest number of people.[9] When discussing the "ethics" of war, this type of example is probably best as modern, democratic governments often "justify" going to war to bring benefit to the greatest number of people. Significantly, in many cases the value of individuals is culturally derived with ethnocentrisms playing a lead role. For example, in the current war in Afghanistan how does one justify the Afghan civilian casualty rate in terms of saving Western lives?

Essentially, ethical dilemmas are resolved through:

1. adherence to your own set of beliefs and values;
2. the probability of a certain outcome; and
3. achieving the greatest good for the greatest number of people (in the "real world" it is hard to determine what course of action actually promotes this end. Different values are often placed on different individuals. If not everyone is considered equal then the concept of the greatest good for the greatest number of people is also put into question).

When resolving an ethical dilemma, you should include:

1. an assessment of the situation;
2. the ethical considerations; and
3. options and risks.[10]

The assessment of the situation concerns the overall environment where the dilemma occurs and includes the perception of facts, concerns, and other issues. *Ethics in the Canadian Forces* describes "facts" as "events or circumstances of the situation itself." Importantly, "they describe the situation as it is *presented to you*."[11] Ethical concerns are identified as "issues that question the ethical nature of the situation, prompting you to perceive some element(s) of the situation as problematic." Personal factors are identified as "personal values, moral responsibilities and the impact of your decision on others and on yourself." Finally, environmental factors "refer to your work — or immediate — environment. It includes perceptions of what is acceptable and unacceptable and what is considered 'your business' and 'none of your business.'" All four areas cover the assessment of the situation.[12]

Once the basics of the situation are identified and assessed, the ethical considerations that frame the situation should be acknowledged. As *Ethics in the Canadian Forces* correctly points out, "They are good indicators of how a situation is perceived, and they assist you in identifying the type of dilemma." The manual identifies the ethical principles of the Canadian Forces as:

1. respect the dignity of all persons (humanity);
2. serve Canada before self (society); and
3. obey and support lawful authority (the rule of the law).[13]

It also identifies the ethical values or the "amalgamation of obligations in which CF members must adhere and are committed to defend" as:

- integrity;
- loyalty;
- courage;
- honesty;
- fairness; and
- responsibility/duty.[14]

The final step prior to committing to an action is to weigh your options and their associated risks. *Ethics in the Canadian Forces* states that "in ethical situations, options are considered the 'best solution' for courses of action and range from acting upon a situation to not-acting."[15] Importantly, the risks that need to be considered can occur at the tactical, operational, and strategic level and should all be taken into consideration before deciding on a course of action.

Given that the COE often requires soldiers to react instantaneously to ambiguous and complex situations, individuals should practise resolving ethical dilemmas prior to deployments. The best way to do so is to analyse case studies and discuss available options using the aforementioned four step model (assessment, ethical considerations, options and risks, and action).[16] Regardless of the practise method, soldiers should be able to quickly identify the situation, the ethical concerns, and the available choices prior to committing to a specific action.

The Ethics of Applying CQ to the COE

As researcher Brooks Peterson remarked, "The ability to work within an ethical framework is a necessary component of cultural intelligence."[17] This statement is even more apt when applied to the complex, ambiguous, volatile, dynamic, and dangerous COE where militaries operate. Nonetheless, the ethical use of CQ is a complicated and difficult task — but not one without some resolution.

In fact, the ethical application of CQ to the COE hinges on two principle concepts. First, act according to your own moral code. Second, understand and respect the host nation population's moral code. While seemingly simple, this is actually a difficult task as the two can be in direct opposition. Ethical dilemmas are sure to occur frequently.

There is no doubt that when using enhanced CQ in the COE it is vitally importance to adhere to your own moral code, even if it is in conflict with that of the opponent. As the *U.S. Army Counterinsurgency Handbook* explains,

> A key part of any insurgents' strategy is to attack the will of the domestic and international opposition. One of the insurgents' most effective ways to undermine and erode political will is to portray their opposition as untrustworthy or illegitimate ... The attacks work especially well when insurgents can portray their opposition as unethical by the opposition's own standards.[18]

As American Major-General (retired) Robert Scales commented, "The enemy clearly understands the war that he's involved in: win and hold cultural high ground — that is his objective — we're playing catch up."[19]

"Holding the cultural high ground" includes being responsible for actions performed by associated surrogate forces as the Americans discovered in 2004 when they closed the Abu Ghraib detention facility due to allegations of misconduct by U.S. Reservists and sent Iraqi prisoners to Iraqi detention facilities that were quickly found to be equally as abusive, and Canadians experienced in 2007 with the Afghan detainee situation.[20] Unsurprisingly, General David McKiernan, commander U.S. Forces in Afghanistan/International Security Assistance Force in Afghanistan, recently advised, "Live our values and act above reproach. Insurgent groups take advantage of our failures and, because they are not constrained by the truth, sometimes our success, too."[21]

For Canadian Forces personnel this means adhering to the previously mentioned ethical principles and ethical values of the CF. *Duty with Honour: The Profession of Arms in Canada* captures the essence of these items as follows: "Canadian military values — which are essential for conducting the full range of military operations, up to and including warfighting — come from what history and experience teach about the importance of moral factors in operations ... These military values are understood and expressed within the Canadian military ethos as follows: Duty ... Loyalty ... Integrity ... Courage ..."[22]

While simultaneously adhering to a Canadian moral code, CF members need to respect the moral code of the host nation population. This is not an altruistic demand but a practical consideration. The *U.S. Cultural Generic Information Requirements Handbook* for the United States Marine Corps states the requirement frankly: "You don't have to like it to understand it ... Some things that we learn about the local culture may anger or puzzle us. That is OK ... View these differences as significant factors that shape the area of operations and affect a unit's ability to carry out missions. Figuring out what is going on (that means getting inside local peoples' heads) may require temporarily suspending your own beliefs, assumptions, and expectations as much as possible to focus on learning over judging." It warns, "This takes mental discipline."[23] However, as Chapters Five and Six of this book explain, it is worth the effort because it can help to win the hearts and minds of host nation populations, often the center of gravity (along with home populations) in the COE.

In summary, the ethics of applying CQ to the COE is an important factor to consider. Essentially, this involves adhering to your own moral code while simultaneously respecting that of the local population. This at times paradoxical commitment can create ethical dilemmas as military members need to decide on the best course of action, of which none are highly desirable and where competing values are often at play. Understanding the nature of ethics, what an ethical dilemma is and the factors to consider when deciding on a course of action (i.e., assessment, ethical considerations, options and risks, and then action) will help military members make ethical choices in a complex and volatile environment. Moreover, these "right decisions" have a practical impact on the outcome of conflict in the COE. Ethically applying CQ is not just the "politically correct" thing to do. It is a force enabler and can be a force multiplier in the COE. CQ can be a powerful tool if used correctly and the ethical employment of CQ is a mandatory step in the right direction.

Notes

Chapter 1

1. This definition of globalization is paraphrased from Professors David Held and Anthony McGrew, who argue that globalization denotes "the expanding scale, growing magnitude, speeding up and deepening impact of transcontinental flows and patterns of social interaction.... It refers to a shift or transformation in the scale of human organization that links distant communities and expands the reach of power relations across the world's regions and continents." David Held and Anthony McGrew, *Globalization/Anti-Globalization: Beyond the Great Divide* (Cambridge: Polity Press, 2002), 1. Notably, there is no real consensus as to the actual definition of globalization or if it is unique to the late twentieth/early twenty-first century. See: Jan Aart Scholte, *Globalization: A Critical Introduction*, Second Edition (Houndmills, U.K.: MacMillan, 2000), and Lui Hebron, and John F. Stack, Jr., *Globalization: Debunking the Myths* (Upper Saddle River, NJ: Pearson/Prentice Hall: 2008).
2. Charles Krulak, "The Strategic Corporal: Leadership in the Three Block War," *Marines Magazine*, January 1999, *www.au.af.mil/au/awc/awcgate/usmc/strategic_corporal.htm*; accessed 25 July 2007.
3. Charles Krulak, "The Three Block War: Fighting in Urban Areas," National Press Club Vital Speeches of the Day, 15 December 1997.
4. Steven Metz and Douglas V. Johnson II, "Asymmetry and U.S. Military Strategy: Definition, Background, and Strategic

Concepts," U.S. Army War College, Strategic Studies Institute, January 2001, 5–6.

5. Colin Gray, "Thinking Asymmetrically in Times of Terror," *Parameters*, Volume 32, No. 1, Spring 2002, 6.

6. Colonel W.J. Fulton, DNBCD, "Capabilities Required of DND, Asymmetric Threats and Weapons of Mass Destruction," Fourth Draft, 18 March 2001, 2/22.

7. "Asymmetric Warfare," Intelligence and Security Encyclopaedia, *www.answers.com/topic/asymmetric-warfare*; accessed 27 June 2010.

8. Colonel Bernd Horn, "From the Cold War to Insurgency: Preparing Leaders for the Contemporary Operating Environment," in Dr. Emily Spencer, *The Difficult War: Perspectives on Insurgency and SOF* (Dundurn/CDA Press, 2009), 200–201.

9. Colonel Bernd Horn, and Thomas X. Hammes, "Modern Warfare Evolves Into a Fourth Generation," *Unrestricted Warfare Symposium*, 2006 Proceedings, 65.

10. General Sir Rupert Smith, *The Utility of Force: the Art of War in the Modern World* (London: Allen Lane, 2005), xiii.

11. William S. Lind "The Changing Face of War: Into the Fourth Generation," *Marine Corps Gazette*, October 1989, 22–26.

12. According to international terrorism expert Walter Laqueur, "Terrorism constitutes the illegitimate use of force to achieve a political objective when innocent people are targeted."

    Former Israeli Prime Minister Benjamin Netanyahu defines terrorism as "the deliberate and systemic assault on civilians to inspire fear for political ends."

    Similarly, Brian Jenkins said, "Terrorism is the use or threatened use of force designed to bring about political change."

    Finally, scholar Michael Walzer insisted, "Terrorism is the random killing of innocent people, in the hope of creating pervasive fear. The fear can serve many political purposes." See Barry Davies, *Terrorism: Inside a World Phenomenon* (London: Virgin, 2003), 14; Benjamin Netanyahu, *Fighting Terrorism: How Democracies can Defeat the International Terrorist* (New York: Noonday Press, 1995), 8; Michael Walzer, "Terrorism and Just

War," *Philosophia*, Volume 34, No. 1 (January 2006), 3; and Horn, "From the Cold War to Insurgency," 199–200.

13. See Colonel Bernd Horn, "Defining Terrorism," in Dr. Emily Spencer, *The Difficult War: Perspectives on Insurgency and SOF* (Toronto: Dundurn/CDA Press, 2009), 111–22.

14. Bernd Horn, "Command and Leadership: Catalyst for Success for Military Operations," *South African Army Vision 2020*. Volume 3. (Pretoria: Institute for Security Studies, 2009, in press).

15. See Bernd Horn, "Outside the Wire — Some Leadership Challenges in Afghanistan," *Canadian Military Journal*, Volume 7, No. 3, Fall 2006, 6–14; and Bernd Horn, *No Lack of Courage: The Epic Tale of Operation Medusa* (Toronto: Dundurn, 2010), Chapters 2 and 8.

16. *Ibid.*

17. *Ibid.* The mujahedeen provide a good example of a group of people who are leveraging modern technology and the cultural gulf between Western and non-Western ways of war to their advantage. The mujahedeen — those who participate in the global jihad — are a group of militants, of which al Qaeda is but one faction, who are determined to establish their goal of strict Islamic rule of the Muslim world. Having established themselves as a group over forty years ago, globalization at the turn of the twenty-first century set the stage for their rise from relative obscurity among laymen to key players in the global arena through their attacks on the United States on 11 September 2001 (9/11). Globalization facilitated the growth of cross-border relationships and strengthened the role of non-state actors on the global stage, as well as providing a forum for the rapid dissemination of information including propaganda. Undoubtedly, 9/11, like 7 December 1941 (the day the Japanese attacked Pearl Harbor), will be a day that will live in infamy among Westerners and has already been described as the date the world changed. From the mujahedeen perspective, the West, and particularly the U.S., have been slowly eroding the cultural integrity of the Muslim world for centuries. Since the 1990s, however, with the

growth of American influence, in part created by the end of the Cold War, this situation has become increasingly viral to the Mujahideed, particularly the U.S. attempt to spread democracy across all regions of the globe. To counter this perceived wrong, the political goal of achieving a new state, *caliphate*, is key to the mujahedeen struggle. One way that they aim to achieve *caliphate* is through prolific writing and the wide distribution of their message facilitated by advanced information technology, such as the Internet. Another means through which they set out to be victorious is through military force, as is the definition of jihad. By committing jihad, the mujahedeen are also able to attack the U.S., and the West economically, by directly attacking resources as well as causing the U.S. to overextend its resources in an attempt to defend its borders and bring the fight to the mujahedeen, a group that, unlike Western nations, is not restrained by national borders. Sarah E. Zabel, *The Military Strategy of Global Jihad* (Carlisle: U.S. Army War College, October 2007), 2–3. Available at *www.strategicstudiesinstitute.army.mil/pdffiles/ PUB809.pdf*; accessed 27 January 2010.

18. Horn, "Command and Leadership."

19. Bernd Horn, "Introduction," *From the Outside Looking In: Media and Defence Analyst Perspectives on Canadian Military Leadership*, (Kingston, ON: CDA Press, 2005), 1.

20. This phenomenon has led to the concept of the "strategic corporal," where the tactical decisions made by junior members on the ground in the glare of media cameras can become strategic issues as they are beamed across the globe by the media in real time, and can influence or incite negative and often violent reactions.

21. See Tom Gjelten, *Professionalism in War Reporting: A Correspondent's View* (New York: Carnegie Commission on Preventing Deadly Conflict, 1998), 2; Evan Thomas, "How a Fire Broke Out," *Newsweek*, 9 and 23 May 2005, 10; and Horn, "Introduction," *From the Outside Looking In*, 1–17.

22. See Tony Balasevicius and Bernd Horn, "Intelligence and its Application to Irregular Warfare," in Dr. Emily Spencer,

The Difficult War: Perspectives on Insurgency and SOF (Toronto: Dundurn/CDA Press, 2009), 53–78.

23. See Dr. Martin Cook, "The Future Operating Environment: Ethical Implications," CCEL 7, 28 November 2006; and Balasevicius and Horn, "Intelligence and Its Implications," 57–61.

24. Angelo M. Codevilla, "Tools of Statecraft: Diplomacy and War," Foreign Policy Research Institute, *www.fpri.org*. In fact, Codevilla goes as far as stating that "Only insofar as a military operation is so crafted as to bring about the desired peace does it qualify as an act of war as opposed to senseless violence."

25. Cited in Christina Mackenzie, "Future Peacekeeping Challenges: Western Europe's Military Chiefs," *Defense News*, 3 April 2000, 34.

26. An example that specifically indicates the Canadian public's desire to have their beliefs, values, and attitudes reflected in the behaviours of their soldiers is the media attention paid in the spring of 2007 to the alleged beatings of Afghan detainees that had been captured by Canadians and released to Afghan authorities. Reporter Licia Corbella remarks on the irony that "the Afghan authorities beat prisoners is hardly surprising when one understands the culture a bit better." Corbella asks, "Isn't that what being a good multiculturalist means? Understanding cultural differences? … Perhaps, thanks in part to Canada, prisons will be one of the first places in Afghanistan where beatings are not the norm. How's that for irony?" Licia Corbella, *Winnipeg Sun*, 2 May 2007, 9.

27. Farewell Message, U.S. Army Chief of Staff General Peter J. Schoomaker, 35th Chief of Staff of the Army.

Chapter 2

1. This section is based primarily on the references provided in the selected bibliography, with an emphasis on the work of Colonel Bernd Horn, with author's permission, as well as the *CANSOFCOM Capstone Concept for Special Operations 2009*.

2. Elitism has always been an emotional issue in most Western democratic societies. The idea of a privileged individual or group in a perceived egalitarian society that embraces the unassailable virtue that all humankind is created equal automatically destroys that illusion. By itself the term creates images of favouritism, privilege, superiority, and standards that are unobtainable by the masses. Within the military it is no different. As Colonel Horn notes, "Universally, military institutions parallel society's outward disdain for elites."

Brigadier-General R.G. Theriault, a former regimental airborne commander, noted that in Canadian society it is not a good thing to produce a group that is favoured above others. The Americans are no different. Thomas Adams, a former director of intelligence and special operations at the U.S. Army Peacekeeping Institute, revealed, "The US military, particularly the Army, has long distrusted the whole idea of elite units on the general principle that such organizations have no place in the armed forces of a democracy."

Martin Kitchen, a professor of history, explained, "The very mention of the idea of a military elite is enough to set the alarm bells ringing in sensitive democratic souls."

Respected military analyst and author Tom Clancy observed, "As always, those who dare rise above the crowd and distinguish themselves will spark envy and resentment."

Similarly, "elitism," acknowledged one former member of an elite unit, "is counter-productive, it alienates you from other people."

See Bernd Horn, "When Cultures Collide: The Conventional Military/SOF Chasm," in Bernd Horn and Tony Balasavecius, eds., *Casting Light on the Shadows: Canadian Perspectives on Special Operations Forces* (Toronto: Dundurn, 2007), 115–46; Thomas K. Adams, *U.S. Special Operations Forces in Action: The Challenge of Unconventional Warfare* (London: Frank Cass, 1998), 9–10; Colonel Bernd Horn, "Love 'Em or Hate 'Em: Learning to Live with Elites," *Canadian Military*

Journal, Vol 8, No. 4, Winter 2007–2008, 32–43; Martin Kitchen, "Elites in Military History," in A. Hamish Ion, and Keith Neilson, eds., *Elite Military Formations in War and Peace* (Wesport, CT: Praeger, 1996), 8; Tom Clancy, *Special Forces* (New York: Berkley Books, 2001), 3; and Andy McNab, *Immediate Action* (London: Bantam Press, 1995), 381.

3. Adams, 162.

4. Julian Thompson, *War Behind Enemy Lines* (Washington, D.C.: Brassey's, 2001), 2.

5. Clancy, *Special Forces*, 3–4.

6. This portion is based on Horn, "When Cultures Collide," and "Love 'Em or Hate 'Em."

7. Philip Warner, *Phantom* (London: William Kimber, 1982), 11.

8. Major-General David Lloyd Owen, *Providence Their Guide: A Personal Account of the Long Range Desert Group* (London: Leo Cooper, 2000), 12.

9. Eric Morris, *Churchill's Private Armies* (London: Hutchinson, 1986), 90.

10. Viscount William Slim, *Defeat Into Victory* (London: Cassell and Company Ltd., 1956), 547. There was a follow-on issue to the "skimming effect." Many commanders perceived negative consequences on those who failed to pass the high standards normally imposed during selection. Alan Brooke and Slim were two of many who were convinced that those rejected had their confidence undermined by failure. Furthermore, the nature of these highly selective units created an impression that everyone else was second-best. But it is more than just an impression; it is a belief. "I was glad they [those not selected] left camp immediately and didn't say any awkward farewells," confessed one SOF operator. "They were social lepers and I didn't want to risk catching the infection they carried."

This attitude is a dangerous one. As one former SAS member noted, "Elitism is counter-productive, it alienates you from other people." Slim, 546; Morris, *Churchill's Private Army*, 243; Command Sergeant Major Eric L. Haney, *Inside Delta Force:*

The Story of America's Elite Counterterrorist Unit (New York: Dell, 2002), 97; and McNab, 381.

11. Brigadier T.B.L. Churchill, "The Value of Commandos," RUSI, Vo 65, No. 577, February 1950, 86.

12. John A. English, *A Perspective on Infantry* (New York: Praeger, 1981), 188.

13. Tom Clancy, *Airborne* (New York: Berkley Books, 1997), 54.

14. See Eliot A. Cohen, *Commandos and Politicians: Elite Military Units in Modern Democracies* (Cambridge, NJ: Center for International Affairs, Harvard University, 1978), 56–58.

15. Slim, 546.

16. Philip Warner, *The SAS: The Official History* (London: Sphere Books, 1971), 1.

17. Tom Clancy, and Fred Franks, *Into the Storm: A Study in Command* (New York: Berkley Books, 1997), 119.

18. Cohen, 61.

19. See Hilary St. George Saunders, *The Green Beret: The Story of the Commandos 1940–1945* (London: Michael Joseph, 1949), 82–101 and 193; and Lieutenant-Colonel Robert D. Burhans, *The First Special Service Force: A War History of the North Americans, 1942–1944* (Toronto: Methuen, 1975), 162; Warner, *Secret Forces*, 17; Adrian Weale, *Secret Warfare: Special Operations Forces From the Great Game to the SAS* (London: Hodder and Stoughton, 1997), 104; Denis and Shelagh Whitaker, *Dieppe: Tragedy to Triumph* (Toronto: McGraw Hill Ryerson, 1992), 48; and A.B. Feuer, *Commando! The M/Z Unit's Secret War Against Japan* (Wesport, CT: Praeger, 1996), 159.

20. Susan L. Marquis, *Unconventional Warfare: Rebuilding U.S. Special Operations Forces* (Washington, D.C.: Brookings Institution Press, 1997), 23.

21. Christopher Hibbert, *Anzio: The Bid for Rome* (New York: Ballatine Books, 1970), 75–76. It must also be noted that SOF is often misemployed. Because they are relatively lightly armed they cannot be used as regular infantry to fight in a conventional manner.

22. John T. Carney, and Benjamin F. Schemmer, *No Room for Error: The Covert Operations of America's Special Tactics Units from Iran to Afghanistan* (New York: Presidio Press Books, 2003), 236, 283.
23. "Ground Troops Cream of Crop," *Toronto Star*, 21 October 2001, A9.
24. Charles A. Cotton, "Military Mystique." (Source Canadian Airborne Forces Museum files — no publication material available.)
25. Cohen, 74.
26. General Sir Peter de la Billiere, *Looking for Trouble: SAS to Gulf Command* (London: Harper Collins, 1995), 117.
27. Eric Morris, *Guerrillas in Uniform: Churchill's Private Armies in the Middle East and the War Against Japan,1940–1945* (London: Hutchinson, 1989), 15.
28. Weale, 154.
29. Cameron Spence, *All Necessary Measures* (London: Penguin Books, 1998), 43.
30. Haney, 20.
31. Anthony Kemp, *The SAS at War: The Special Air Service Regiment 1941–1945* (London: John Murray, 1991), 11.
32. Charles M. Simpson III, *Inside the Green Berets: The First Thirty Years* (Novato, CA: Presidio, 1983), 14; and Charles W. Sasser, *Raider* (New York: St. Martins, 2002), 186.
33. Simpson III, 14; Sasser, 186.
34. Simpson III, 21.
35. De la Billiere, 236.
36. *Ibid.*, 98.
37. Greg Jaffe, "A Maverick's Plan to Revamp Army is Taking Shape," *Wall Street Journal*, 12 December 2003.
38. John Talbot, "The Myth and Reality of the Paratrooper in the Algerian War," *Armed Forces and Society*, November 1976, 75; Cohen, 69; and Donna Winslow, *The Canadian Airborne Regiment in Somalia: A Socio-cultural Inquiry* (Ottawa: Commission of Inquiry into the Deployment of Canadian Forces to Somalia, 1997), 135–41.

39. Spence, 43.
40. Quoted in Horn, "A Cultural Divide."
41. *Ibid*.
42. Winslow, 126–33.
43. Allan Bell, formerly of 22 SAS, Presentation to the RMC Special Operations Symposium, 5 October 2000.
44. Clancy, *Special Forces*, 281.
45. Colonel J.W. Hackett, "The Employment of Special Forces," *RUSI*, Vol 97, No. 585, February 1952, 41.
46. Colin S. Gray, *Explorations in Strategy* (London: Greenwood Press, 1996), 151, 156.
47. Aaron Bank, *From OSS to Green Berets: The Birth of Special Forces* (Novato, CA: Presidio, 1986), 147.
48. Quoted in Susan L. Marquis, *Unconventional Warfare: Rebuilding U.S. Special Operations Forces* (Washington, D.C.: Brookings Institution Press, 1997), 6.
49. Hackett, 35.
50. *Ibid*., 39.
51. *Ibid*., 39.
52. One need only look at recent pictures from Afghanistan or Iraq to understand. Long hair, beards, no rank epaulets, no military headdress (although ball caps are often a favourite), mixed dress (civilian and military), fashionable sunglasses, and an array of exotic weaponry and equipment give away the SOF operator.
53. Major-General Tony Jeapes, *SAS Secret War* (Surrey: The Book People Ltd., 1996), 12.
54. Quoted in Marquis, 7.
55. Will Fowler, *The Commandos at Dieppe: Rehearsal for D-Day* (London: Harper Collins, 2002), 29.
56. John Leary, "Searching for a Role: The Special Air Service (SAS) Regiment in the Malayan Emergency," *Army Historical Research*, Vol 63, No. 296, Winter 1996, 269.
57. This segment is based primarily on Bernd Horn, "Love 'Em or Hate 'Em: Learning to Live with Elites," *Canadian Military Journal*, Vol 8, No. 4, Winter 2007–2008, 32–43, with author's permission.

58. E. Aronson and J. Mills, "The Effect of Severity of Initiation on Liking for a Group," *Journal of Abnormal & Social Psychology*, 1957, 157–58. Elliot Aronson of Stanford University and Judson Mills of the U.S. Army Leadership and Human Research Unit established this in their 1959 laboratory experiments. They stated, "Subjects who underwent a severe initiation perceived the group as being significantly more attractive than those who underwent a mild or no initiation." See also R.B. Cialdini, *Influence: Science and Practise*, third edition. (Arizona: Harper Collins, 1993), 70 and 74; and Major James McCollum, "The Airborne Mystique," *Military Review*, Vol 56, No. 11, November 1976, 16.

59. W.D. Henderson, *Cohesion: The Human Element in Combat* (Washington, D.C.: National Defence University Press, 1985), 14.

60. Elmar Dinter, *Hero or Coward: Pressures Facing the Soldier in Battle* (London: Frank Cass, 1985), 41; and Anthony Kellet, *Combat Motivation: The Behavior of Soldiers in Battle* (Boston: Kluwer-Nijhoff Publishing, 1982), 45–46.

61. Linda Robinson, *Masters of Chaos: The Secret History of the Special Forces* (New York: Public Affairs, 2004), xx.

62. The following section on SOF theory is based on CANSOFCOM's doctrinal publication: *Canada, CANSOFCOM Capstone Concept for Special Operations 2009* (draft), (Ottawa: DND, 2009).

63. William Walker, "Shadow Warriors: Elite Troops Hunt Terrorists in Afghanistan," *Toronto Star*, 20 October 2001, A4.

64. Tom Clancy, *Special Forces* (New York: Berkley Books, 2001), 3.

65. Special operations differ from conventional operations in the degree of physical and political risk, operational techniques, modes of employment, independence from friendly support, and dependence on detailed operational intelligence.

66. CANSOFCOM is composed of command headquarters (i.e., command cell, chief of staff [COS] operations, COS Support, and COS Force Development), Joint Task Force 2, Canadian Special Operations Regiment, and 427 Special Operations Aviation Squadron.

67. The original author of the SOF Truths was Colonel John M. Collins. He noted the "Fifth" SOF Truth has been completely ignored by the international SOF community.

68. JTF 2 was created in 1992 and took over responsibilities for the national hostage rescue/counter-terrorism role from the Royal Canadian Mounted Police (RCMP) Special Emergency Response Team (SERT) in 1993. It was Canada's only SOF force until the creation of CANSOFCOM.

69. HVT tasks are defined as follows:

Special Reconnaissance (SR), are missions conducted to collect or verify information of strategic or operational significance. These actions complement and refine other collection methods but are normally directed upon extremely significant areas of interest.

Direct Action (DA), are short duration strikes and other precise small-scale offensive actions conducted by special operation forces to seize, destroy, capture, exploit, recover, or damage designated targets. Direct action differs from conventional offensive actions in the level of physical and political risk, operational techniques, and the degree of discriminate and precise use of force to achieve specific objectives.

Counter-proliferation (CP), are actions to limit the possession, use, acquisition, or transit of weapons of mass effect (WME). It includes actions to locate, seize, capture, and recover WME and in some instances under the Proliferation Security Initiative prevent the improper employment of dual use materials.

Non-Combatant Evacuation Operations (NEO), are operations that are conducted to assist the Department of Foreign Affairs in the evacuations of Canadians from foreign host nations. SOTF can play a key supporting role through the provision of early special reconnaissance, providing strategic communications links and security advice.

Defence, Diplomacy, and Military Assistance (DDMA), are operations that contribute to nation building through assistance to select states through the provision of specialized military advice, training, and assistance (e.g., CPAT, MTAP). CANSOFCOM contributions are managed within the Command's areas of expertise.

Chapter 3

1. Lieutenant-Colonel Ian Hope, in a professional development presentation for the Canadian Forces Leadership Institute at the Canadian Defence Academy, Kingston, ON, November 2006.
2. Cited in Frank G. Hoffman, "Principles for the Savage Wars of Peace," in Anthony McIvor, ed., *Rethinking the Principles of War* (Annapolis, MD: Naval Institute Press, 2005), 304.
3. Brigadier-General David Fraser, former commander, ISAF Multi-National Brigade Sector South, Kandahar, Afghanistan, presentation to Canadian Infantry Association Annual General Meeting, Edmonton, 25 May 2007.
4. Robert H. Scales cited in Helen Altman Klein and Gilbert Kuperman, "Through an Arab Cultural Lens," *Military Review*, May/June 2008, 100.
5. There are several different terminologies used to express the advantageous use of cultural knowledge. These terms include, but are not limited to, cultural savvy, cultural astuteness, cultural literacy, cultural appreciation, cultural expertise, human terrain, cultural awareness, cultural competency, and cross-cultural competence. There are also many different proposed acronyms for cultural intelligence, for example, CI, CULTINT, and CQ.

    CQ draws parallels to the more commonly used term intelligence quotient (IQ). IQ is based on the early twentieth century findings of German psychologist William Stern that the mental age to chronological age remains relatively constant throughout ones life. This suggests that an individual's IQ does not change throughout his or her lifetime. "What Does IQ Stand for and What does it Mean?" *www.geocities.com/rnseitz/Definition_of_ IQ.html*; accessed 14 July 2007.

However, the way that CQ is used in this chapter directly argues that individuals can increase their CQ with knowledge and the motivation to apply that knowledge toward a specific goal. Indeed, P. Christopher Earley and Soon Ang, the originators of the term, are also clear on this point. They write, "We use the shorthand label of CQ as a convenience to remind the reader that this is a facet of intelligence. However, we do not use CQ in a strict fashion as is implied by 'IQ'; that is, we do not mean to denote a mathematical relationship generated from normative data of capability. In this sense, our usage parallels that from the literature on emotional intelligence and their usage of 'EQ.'" P. Christopher Earley, and Soon Ang, *Cultural Intelligence: Individual Interactions Across Cultures* (Stanford: Stanford Business Books, 2003), 4.

Cultural intelligence and the acronym CQ were chosen for this chapter for the same reason that Early and Ang chose to use the term: CQ stresses the intelligence component of cultural intelligence. Notably, CQ does not limit the concept to a strictly mathematical calculation of a static competency. Moreover, whatever the label one applies to the concept, in the end the key is to determine what enables people to function effectively in cultural settings.

6. Ben Connable, "All Our Eggs in a Broken Basket: How the Human Terrain System is Undermining Sustainable Military Cultural Competence," *Military Review*, March/April 2009, 58.

7. Henri Bore, "Complex Operations in Africa: Operational Culture Training in the French Military," *Military Review*, March/April 2009, 70.

8. Both CQ and the Four CQ Domain Paradigm will be further explained in subsequent chapters.

9. Jacob Kipp, Lester Grau, Karl Prinslow, and Don Smith, "The Human Terrain System: A CORDS for the 21st Century," *Military Review*, September/October 2006, 8.

10. Cited in George W. Smith, "Avoiding a Napoleonic Ulcer: Bridging the Gap of Cultural Intelligence," *A Common Perspective*, May 2006, Vol 14, No. 1, 23. *www.dtic.mil/doctrine/jel/comm_per/common_perspective.htm*; accessed 16 July 2009.

11. Philip Taylor cited in Tony Skinner, "Shaping Influence," *Jane's Defence Quarterly*, 23 August 2006, 29.

12. Farewell Message, U.S. Army Chief of Staff General Peter J. Schoomaker, 35th Chief of Staff of the Army.

13. Lieutenant Ian Hope, "Reflections on Afghanistan: Commanding Task Force Orion," in Bernd Horn, ed., *In Harm's Way*, Vol. II: *The Buck Stops Here: Senior Commanders on Operations* (Winnipeg: Canadian Defence Academy Press, 2007), 211.

14. Robert Scales, testifying before the House of Armed Services Committee, 15 July, 2004, *www.au.af.mil/au/awc/awcgate/congress/04-07-15scales.pdf*.

15. Kipp *et al.*, "The Human Terrain System," 9.

16. Benjamin T. Delp, "Ethnographic Intelligence (ETHNINT) and Cultural Intelligence (CULINT): Employing Under-utilized Strategic Intelligence Gathering Disciplines for More Effective Diplomatic and Military Planning," *IIIA Technical Paper 08-02*, April 2008, 2.

17. Cited in George W. Smith, "Avoiding a Napoleonic Ulcer," 11.

18. Cited in Montgomery McFate, "The Military Utility of Understanding Adversary Culture," *Joint Force Quarterly*, 38, 2005, 43.

19. *Ibid.*

20. *Ibid.*, 43–44.

21. *Ibid.*, 45.

22. *Ibid.*, 48.

23. Bill Edmonds, "A Soldier's Story," posted online, 29 November 2006, *www.thenation.com/doc/20061211/soldiers_story*.

24. P.M. Zeman, "Goat-Grab: Diplomacy in Iraq," *Proceedings*, November 2005, 20.

25. Lorenzo Puertas, "Corporal Jones and the Moment of Truth," *Proceedings*, November 2004, 44.

26. The NATO definition for information operations is "Info Ops is a military function to provide advice and co-ordination of military information activities in order to create desired effects on the will, understanding and capability of adversaries, potential adversaries

and other NAC approved parties in support of Alliance mission objectives." Cited in Colonel W.N. Peters (Retired), *Shifting to the Moral Plane: The Canadian Approach to Information Operations* (Kingston, ON: Canadian Forces Leadership Institute Technical Report, 2007), 20–21.

27. Cited in Skinner, "Shaping Influence," 24.
28. Thomas Metz cited in *Ibid.*, 26.
29. *Ibid.*, 27.
30. Bore, "Complex Operations in Africa," 69.
31. Puertas, "Corporal Jones and the Moment of Truth," 43.
32. Roger Noble, "The Essential Thing: Mission Command and its Practical Application," *Command Papers*, Australian Defence College, May 2007, 4.
33. The concept of the "strategic corporal," refers to cases where the tactical decisions made by junior members on the ground in the glare of media cameras can become strategic issues as they are beamed across the globe by the media in real time and influence or incite often negative and potentially violent reactions.
34. Bernd Horn, ed., *From the Outside Looking In: Media and Defence Analyst Perspectives on Canadian Military Leadership* (Kingston, ON: Canadian Defence Academy Press, 2005), 1.
35. Major-General Andrew Leslie (Deputy Commander ISAF, 2002), CFLI interview with Colonel Bernd Horn, 8 February 2006.
36. Major-General Robert Scales, presentation at "Cognitive Dominance Workshop," West Point, 11 July 2006.

Chapter 4

1. Lieutenant-Colonel Ian Hope in a professional development presentation for the Canadian Forces Leadership Institute at the Canadian Defence Academy, Kingston, ON, November 2006.
2. Allan D. English, *Understanding Military Culture: A Canadian Perspective* (Montreal: McGill-Queen's University Press, 2004), 12.

Notably, there is long-standing debate about the nature and definition of culture. The current 2006 American counter-insurgency manual, for example, contrasts cultural and social structures. It explains: "Social structure comprises the relationships among groups, institutions, and individuals within a society; in contrast, culture (ideas, norms, rituals, codes of behaviour) provide meaning to individuals within the society." It defines culture as a "'web of meaning' shared by members of a particular society or group within a society." The manual explains this definition in terms of people's identity, beliefs, values, attitudes, perceptions, and belief systems. It also emphasize that cultural knowledge about insurgents, as far as the military is concerned, should be exploited to be used to further U.S. national objectives. *Counterinsurgency*, 3–6, 3–8. Similarly, scholar Adam Bozeman, defines culture as "Those norms, values, institutions and modes of thinking in a given society that survive change and remain meaningful to successive generations." Adda Bozeman, cited in Montgomery McFate, "The Military Utility of Understanding Adversary Culture," *Joint Force Quarterly*, 38, 2005, 48, note 4. While all these definitions (as well as most of the available definitions of culture) are complementary, English's does an exceptional job of breaking culture down into its component parts and thereby making the concept of culture more understandable at a structural level. For this reason, this definition is expanded on and returned to in discussions of culture and cultural intelligence.

3. Adapted from English, *Understanding Military Culture*, 12.
4. *Ibid.*, 11–12.
5. *Ibid.*, 11.
6. *Ibid.*, 12–14.
7. Center for Advanced Operational Culture Learning (CAOCL), *Afghanistan: Operational Culture for Deploying Personnel* (CAOCL: Quantico, August 2006), 8.
8. English, *Understanding Military Culture*, 24.
9. Geopolitics looks at the relationships between politics, economics, and geography, both human and physical.

10. Samuel P. Huntington, *The Clash of Civilizations: Remaking of World Order* (New York: Simon & Schuster, 1996), 29.
11. Huntington, *The Clash of Civilizations*, 21.
12. *Ibid.*
13. *Ibid.*
14. Janet A. Simons, Donald B. Irwin, and Beverly A. Drinnien, *Psychology: The Search for Understanding* (New York: West Publishing Company, 1987), *honolulu.hawaii.edu/intranet/committees/FacDevCom/guidebk/teachtip/maslow.htm*; accessed 17 July 2007.
15. Hofstede's four value dimensions are described in Martin M. Chemers, *An Integrative Theory of Leadership* (Mahwah, NJ: Lawrence Erlbaum Associates, 1997). Hofstede has also published extensively and has added a fifth value dimension to his list: long-term orientation. This last dimension explores the differences between long-term goals expressed through economic thrift and perseverance and those that are more immediate, such as respect for tradition, committing to social obligations, and saving face.
16. Notably, some individuals create formalised categories whereas many simply intrinsically describe value dimensions. For an example of the former see Henri Bore, "Complex Operations in Africa: Operational Culture Training in the French Military," *Military Review*, March–April 2009, 65–71. Interestingly, many of these cultural "models" have overlapping dimensions.
17. See the chapter on fear by Bernd Horn in Bernd Horn and Robert W. Walker, (eds.), *The Military Leadership Handbook* (Toronto: Dundurn/CDA Press, 2008); and Bernd Horn, "Revisiting the Worm: An Examination of Fear and Courage," *Canadian Military Journal 5* (2004), 5–16.

Chapter 5

1. P. Christopher Earley and Elaine Mosakowski, "Cultural Intelligence," *Harvard Business Review* October (2004), 139–40.

2. Earley and Ang, *Cultural Intelligence: Individual Interactions Across Cultures*, 59, 67.

3. Earley and Peterson, "The Elusive Cultural Chameleon," 105.

4. Johnson, Lenartowicz, and Apud, "Cross-Cultural Competence in International Business," 525–44; Thomas, "Domains and Development of Cultural Intelligence: The Importance of Mindfulness," 78–96.

5. Earley and Ang, *Cultural Intelligence*, 12.

6. *Ibid.*, 94.

7. Carol McCann cited in Chris Thatcher, "Forecasting Adversarial Intent: Unravelling the Human Dimension."

8. Leonard Wong, Stephen Gerras, William Kidd, Robert Pricone, and Richard Swengros, "Strategic Leadership Competencies," *Report*, U.S. Department of the Army, 7.

9. U.S. Directorate of Research, Center for Advanced Defense Studies, "Oracles of Intelligence," Defense Concepts Series, July 2006.

10. *Cultural Generic Information Requirements Handbook* (C-GIRH), DoD-GIRH-2634-001-08, 2.

11. John P. Coles, "Incorporating Cultural Intelligence Into Joint Doctrine," *IO Sphere: Joint Information Operation Center*, Spring 2006, 7. This definition is also used by researcher Benjamin T. Delp in Benjamin T. Delp, "Ethnographic Intelligence (ETHNINT) and Cultural Intelligence (CULINT): Employing Under-utilized Strategic Intelligence Gathering Disciplines for More Effective Diplomatic and Military Planning," *IIIA Technical Paper 08-02*, April 2008, 4.

12. Henri Bore, "Complex Operations in Africa: Operational Culture Training in the French Military," *Military Review*, March–April 2009, 65.

13. This definition as well as the concept of the four CQ domain paradigm was developed by the author after consulting multiple sources that explore CQ.

14. Interview Colonel Fred Lewis by Adam Day, *Legion Magazine*, November 2006.

15. Licia Corbella, *Winnipeg Sun*, 2 May 2007, 9.

16. A recent Department of National Defence report states that "standing [with the Canadian public] of the Canadian Forces has clearly risen since the Somalia scandal thanks to a general alignment between military values and Canadian values." Cited in Allan Woods, *Toronto Star*, 19 May 2007.

17. See Horn, "Full Spectrum Leadership," 206–207; Sayed Salahuddin, "Airstrikes Kill Scores of Afghan Civilians," Yahoo News, *news.yahoo.com/s/nm/20070707/wl_nm/afghan_violence_dc_3*; accessed 7 Jul 2007; Greg Weston, "Battle for Public Opinion Desire to have Troops Withdraw from Combat in Afghanistan Growing, Polls Show," *Winnipeg Sun*, 24 Jun 2007, 13; and "Opposition Leaders Unite as War Toll Mounts," *Edmonton Sun*, 5 Jul 2007, 38.

18. Michael Ignatieff, *Virtual War: Ethical Challenges* (Annapolis: United States Naval Academy, March 2001), 7.

19. Lieutenant-General James N. Mattis, *Ethical Challenges in Contemporary Conflict: The Afghanistan and Iraq Cases* (Annapolis: United States Naval Academy, March 2001), 11.

20. Command is generally accepted by the military community to mean "the authority vested in an individual of the armed forces for the direction, co-ordination, and control of military forces." Canada, *Command* (Ottawa: DND, 1997), 4. This is the NATO doctrinal definition.

21. Organizational chains of command may seem to supersede even national command in theatre. For instance, both the Department of National Defence (DND) and the Department of Foreign Affairs and International Trade (DFAIT) have personnel serving in Afghanistan. Both departments are serving the Canadian government, yet commanders and managers on the ground have responsibilities to both their immediate in-situ commanders/directors and to their superiors in Ottawa. This can obscure and work against the unity of command as departmental agendas and rivalries begin to interfere with actions in theatre.

22. Bernd Horn, "Full Spectrum Leadership Challenges in Afghanistan," in Horn, ed., *In Harm's Way*, Vol. II: *The Buck Stops Here*, 197–98.
23. Carol McCann cited in Chris Thatcher, "Forecasting Adversarial Intent: Unravelling the Human Dimension."
24. Adnan R. Khan, "I'm Here to Fight: Canadian Troops in Kandahar," *Maclean's*, 5 April 2006, *www.macleans.ca/article.jsp?co ntent=20060403_124448_124448*; accessed 18 July 2006.
25. Edmonds, "A Soldier's Story."
26. David McKiernan, "COMISAF Counterinsurgency Guidance," *The Enduring Ledger*, April 2009, 8–9.
27. *Ibid.*, 10.
28. Interviews conducted by Dr. Emily Spencer at Canadian Forces Base Edmonton, January 2007.

Chapter 6

1. See Peter C. Newman, *Canadian Revolution 1985–1995: From Deference to Defiance* (Toronto: Viking Press, 1995). For an account of the impact of the changes to the CF in the 1990s, see Bernd Horn, *Bastard Sons: An Examination of Canada's Airborne Experience, 1942–1995* (St. Catharines, ON: Vanwell), 201; Bernd Horn and Bill Bentley, "The Road to Transformation: Ascending from the Decade of Darkness," in R.W. Walker, ed., *Institutional Leadership in the Canadian Forces: Contemporary Issues* (Kingston, ON: CDA Press, 2007), 1–25; and "An Absence of Honour," in Alister MacIntyre and Karen Davis, eds., *Dimensions of Military Leadership*. (Kingston, ON: CDA Press, 2007), 245–80.
2. Seventy-one percent of Canadians said "no" to any extension of the mission in Afghanistan past the scheduled departure in 2011. Despite the Harper Conservative Government's "hawkish" approach to military affairs, in light of the overwhelming public sentiment they have stuck to the withdrawal pledge.

Ipsos-Reid/CanWest Global Afghanistan Mission, January 2009 poll. DND, "Public Opinion Research," Presentation to PAPCT, 28 January 2009.

3. See Russell D. Howard, "Intelligence in Denied Areas. New Concepts for A Changing Environment," JSOU Report 07-10, December 2007.

4. DDMA is the Canadian version of Foreign Internal Defence (FID) in the American lexicon. FID has been replaced by the term Security Force Assistance (SFA). CQ is also pivotal in unconventional warfare (UW).

5. See Richard D. Newton, Travis L. Homiak, Kelly H. Smith, Isaac J. Peltier, and D. Jonathan White, *Contemporary Security Challenges: Irregular Warfare and Indirect Approaches*, JSOU Report 09-3, February 2009.

6. Adrian T. Bogart III, "Block by Block: Civic Action in the Battle of Baghdad," Joint Special Operations University (JSOU) Report 07-08, November 2007, 5.

7. It is not uncommon for rivals to denounce their competitors as Taliban or al Qaeda or simply as terrorists in order to have the Coalition remove their business (criminal or otherwise) rivals from the scene.

Chapter 7

1. Robert Scales, testifying before the House of Armed Services Committee, 15 July 2004, 5. *www.au.af.mil/au/awc/awcgate/ congress/04-07-15scales.pdf*.

2. Thomas Metz cited in Tony Skinner, "Shaping Influence," *Jane's Defence Quarterly*, 23 August 2006, 27–26. Although Metz commented in 2006, arguably his assessment is equally as true today.

3. Ben Connable, "All Our Eggs in a Broken Basket: How the Human Terrain System is Undermining Sustainable Military Cultural Competence," *Military Review*, March/April 2009, 58.

4. Stanley McChrystal, "Tactical Directive," Headquarters ISAF, Kabul, Afghanistan, 6 July 2009.

5. Gregory Fontenot, "Seeing Red: Creating a Red-Team Capability for the Blue Force," *Military Review*, September–October 2005, 4.

6. John Conrad, *What the Thunder Said: Reflections of a Canadian Officer in Kandahar* (Kingston, ON: CDA Press/Dundurn Press, 2009), 41.

7. Stanley McChrystal, "Tactical Directive," Headquarters ISAF, Kabul, Afghanistan, 6 July 2009.

8. Ronald Haycock, cited in Bernd Horn, "Soldier/Scholar: An Irreconcilable Divide?" *The Army Doctrine and Training Bulletin*, Vol 4, No. 4, Winter 2001–2002, 4

9. David Last, cited in *Ibid.*

10. John Cowan cited in *Ibid.*, 5.

11. *Ibid.*, 7.

12. S.J. Rachman, *Fear and Courage* (San Francisco: W.H.Freeman and Company, 1978), 63–64.

13. Robert Lyman, *Slim, Master of War* (London: Constable, 2004), 78.

14. The Critical Thinking Community, "Critical Thinking as Defined by the National Council for Excellence in Critical Thinking, 1987" *www.criticalthinking.org/aboutct/define_critical_thinking.cfm*; accessed 18 February 2010.

15. Some argue that you can directly teach people how to think (i.e., critical thinking). See Alec Fischer, *Critical Thinking: An Introduction* (Cambridge, U.K.: Cambridge University Press, 2001). While Fischer is correct to claim that certain skills pertain to critical thinking can be taught (i.e., how to structure an argument, judge credibility of a source, or make a decision), as critical thinking is such a personal endeavour and one that applies to all walks of life, I feel that one has to learn for themselves how to apply the aforementioned thinking skills to their lives. As such, it is not really taught, although an understanding of thinking skills is a foundation, as it is integrated into peoples daily lives and the fibre of their beings.

16. In this context, "fact" and "truth" remain elusive concepts.

17. The Critical Thinking Community, "Critical Thinking as Defined by the National Council for Excellence in Critical Thinking, 1987" *www.criticalthinking.org/aboutct/define_critical_thinking.cfm*.

18. Adapted from *Ibid*.

19. *Ibid*.

20. See for example, Milan Zafirovski, "What is Really Rational Choice? Beyond the Utilitarian Concept of Rationality," *Current Sociology* (1999) Vol. 47, No. 1: 47–113.

21. Carol McCann cited in Chris Thatcher, "Forecasting Adversarial Intent: Unravelling the Human Dimension."

22. For more details on these dimensions see Chapter Four. Hofstede's four value dimensions are described in Martin M. Chemers, *An Integrative Theory of Leadership* (Mahwah, NJ: Lawrence Erlbaum Associates, 1997).

23. James A. Bates, *The War on Terrorism: Countering Global Insurgency in the 21st Century*. JSOU Report 05-8, December 2005 (Hurlburt Field, FL: JSOU Press, 2005), 5.

24. Jacob Kipp, Lester Grau, Karl Prinslow, and Don Smith, "The Human Terrain System: A CORDS for the 21st Century," *Military Review*, September–October 2006, 9. Notably, the U.S. Army Combined Arms Center suggests that a broad education in the social sciences is best for effective operations in the COE. They encourage study in the disciplines of history, philosophy, anthropology, sociology, political science, literature, comparative religions, economics, languages, geography, rhetoric, and art and music. *Counterinsurgency Fundamental "Snap Shot."*

25. Henri Bore, "Complex Operations in Africa: Operational Culture Training in the French Military," *Military Review*, March–April 2009, 68.

26. Robert Scales, testifying before the House of Armed Services Committee, 15 July 2004, *www.au.af.mil/au/awc/awcgate/congress/04-07-15scales.pdf*.

27. Benjamin C. Freakley cited in Kipp *et al.*, "The Human Terrain System," 9.

28. Robert Scales, testifying before the House of Armed Services Committee, 15 July 2004, *www.au.af.mil/au/awc/awcgate/congress/04-07-15scales.pdf.*

29. Henri Bore, "Complex Operations in Africa: Operational Culture Training in the French Military," *Military Review*, March–April 2009, 71.

30. Prisco R. Hernandez, "Developing Cultural Understanding in Stability Operations: A Three-Step Process," *Field Artillery*, January–February 2007, 6.

31. David Segal cited in Edward J. Healey Jr., *Cultural Competency Training in the United States Marine Corps: A Prescription for Success in the Long War*, M.A. Thesis (Fort Leavenworth: U.S. Army Command and General Staff College, 2008), 15.

    This lag in competencies also applies to intelligence preparation of the battlefield. As Benjamin Delp, assistant director for policy and administration at the Institute for Infrastructure and Information Assurance at James Madison University, commented in his discussion of the importance of CQ to the COE, "The emphasis should be on strong collection strategies prior to engaging an enemy on hostile, non-Western terra." He warned, "It would be a mistake … to overlook the value of these intelligence disciplines [ethnographic intelligence and cultural intelligence] *before* military operations commence in other 'hotspots.'" Benjamin T. Delp in Benjamin T. Delp, "Ethnographic Intelligence (ETHNINT) and Cultural Intelligence (CULINT): Employing Under-utilized Strategic Intelligence Gathering Disciplines for More Effective Diplomatic and Military Planning," *IIIA Technical Paper 08-02*, April 2008, 17.

32. Richard D. Newton, "The Seeds of Surrogate Warfare," in Richard D. Newton, Travis L. Homiak, Kelly H. Smith, Isaac J. Peltier, and D. Jonathan White, *Contemporary Security Challenges: Irregular Warfare and Indirect Approaches*, JSOU Report 09-3, February 2009 (Hurlburt Field, FL: JSOU Press, 2009), 3–4.

33. Montgomery McFate, "The Military Utility of Understanding Adversary Culture," *Joint Force Quarterly*, 38, 2005, 47.

34. Every soldier and officer needs to know that cultural intelligence is an important force multiplier. They need to appreciate that applying enhanced CQ to the COE is operationally effective, not just "politically correct."

35. Education should be available to all military members regardless of rank or occupation and selection for specialized education should be based on aptitude and performance in learning. See Scales, testifying before the House of Armed Services Committee, 15 July 2004, *www.au.af.mil/au/awc/awcgate/congress/04-07-15scales.pdf*.

36. The importance of language to culture has recently been underscored. For example, researcher Clifford F. Porter wrote, "Truly 'knowing our enemy' requires understanding the culture, politics, and religion of the terrorists, which in turn requires experts in their language. Two earlier lessons learned from Afghanistan are that foreign language skills were absolutely critical for overthrowing the Taliban regime so quickly and that the military does not have enough foreign language capability." Clifford F. Porter, *Asymmetrical Warfare, Transformation, and Foreign Language Capability*. Army Command and General Staff College (Fort Leavenworth, KS: Combat Studies Institute, 2006). See also, Hernandez, "Developing Cultural Understanding in Stability Operations."

37. That is not to say that cultural understanding should be farmed out to contractors. Human terrain systems (HTSs) and human terrain teams (HTTs) are steps that the Americans are taking to help bridge the cultural gap. D. Jonathan White explains, "The United States has attempted to improve the cultural knowledge of U.S. forces conducting counterinsurgency in Iraq and Afghanistan by employing human terrain teams (HTTs). HTTs consist of anthropologists, political scientists, or historians that possess or build knowledge of the culture in which the U.S. forces operate." However, the verdict about their utility has yet to be determined. White continues, "This knowledge is certainly important in conducting effective counterinsurgency operations, yet the importation of foreign HTT members into

a culture provides maneuver commanders with a form of artificial knowledge of the culture in which U.S. forces are operating. This knowledge is artificial because it is exogenous and must be built over time by the HTTs." D. Jonathan White, "Legitimacy and Surrogate Warfare," in Richard D. Newton, Travis L. Homiak, Kelly H. Smith, Isaac J. Peltier, and D. Jonathan White, *Contemporary Security Challenges: Irregular Warfare and Indirect Approaches*, JSOU Report 09-3, February 2009 (Hurlburt Field, FL: JSOU Press, 2009), 89.

For further discussion on the debate about HTS see Kipp *et al.* "The Human Terrain System: A CORDS for the 21st Century," and Connable, "All Our Eggs in a Broken Basket: How the Human Terrain System is Undermining Sustainable Military Cultural Competence." While the verdict may still be out on the utility of HTS and HTTs with respect to SOF, there is no doubt that they require an organic growth of CQ within their ranks. As such, while experts may be called upon to help with education and training, there is no substitute for imparting the knowledge to SOF personnel.

38. In essence, "red teaming" involves one group of people acting as the adversary. According to military affairs analyst Williamson Murray, writing for the Defense Adaptive Red Team, red teaming "provide[s] a means to build intellectual constructs that replicate how the enemy thinks [because the constructs] rest on a deep intellectual understanding of his culture, [the] ideological (or religious) framework through which he interprets the world (including the battlefield) and his possible and potential strategic and operational moves. Such red teaming is of considerable importance in estimating the nature of the future battlefield. But it might be even more important in providing military leaders and staff officers a wider and deeper understanding of how the enemy will fight." Williamson Murray cited in Gregory Fontenot, "Seeing Red: Creating a Red-Team Capability for the Blue Force," 5.

In the Canadian context, Defence Research Development Canada is also improving its ability to "red team." According to

Carol McCann, this task "requires expertise in culture, but it also requires imagination, and the ability to challenge in a constructive way." Carol McCann cited in Chris Thatcher, "Forecasting Adversarial Intent: Unravelling the Human Dimension."

39. Henri Bore, "Complex Operations in Africa: Operational Culture Training in the French Military," *Military Review*, March–April 2009, 71.

Chapter 8

1. The BBC website on the "Religion and Ethics: Ethical Issues" describes a just war as follows: "A war is only just if it is fought for a reason that is justified, and that carries sufficient moral weight. The country that wishes to use military force must demonstrate that there is a just cause to do so. The main just cause is to put right a wrong. Sometimes a war fought to prevent a wrong from happening may be considered a just war. In modern times wars to defend the innocent are increasingly regarded as just (which fits with the idea in some religious literature that it is better to defend an innocent than to defend oneself)." *www.bbc.co.uk/ethics/war/just/cause_1.shtml.*

   According to the *Stanford Encyclopaedia of Philosophy*, just war theory contends that for any war to be justified a political community, or state, must fulfill each and every one of the following six requirements: just cause, right intention, proper authority and public declaration, last resort, probability of success, and proportionality. Brian Orend, "War," in *Stanford Encyclopaedia of Philosophy*, accessible at *plato.stanford.edu/entries/war/#2.*

   While these definitions appear to be straightforward, they hinge on what people consider "just" or "moral" and these sentiments are not universal. Consequently, at least one adversary will likely consider their side just, but although they differ in motives and intentions, more than one side can consider their position just.

See also Michael Walzer, *Just and Unjust Wars: A Moral Argument with Historical Illustrations* (New York: Basic Books, 1977).

2. Robert G. Spulak. "A Theory of Special Operations: The Origin, Qualities, and Use of SOF," JSOU Report 07-10, October 2007 (Hulburt Field, FL: JSOU Press, 2007), 6.

3. Notably, there are different types of ethics. Normative ethics refer to how people ought to behave whereas descriptive ethics deals with how we actually do behave. As Harold H. Titus, Marilyn S. Smith, and Richard T. Nolan describe, "In descriptive ethics we consider the conduct of individuals — or personal morality — and of groups — or social morality. We analyze the wide range of human conduct, which includes motives, intentions, and overt acts. This purely descriptive examination is distinguished from normative ethics, which is concerned with the principles by which we *ought* to live." Harold H. Titus, Marilyn S. Smith, and Richard T. Nolan, *Living Issues in Philosophy*, Eighth Edition (Belmont, KY: Wadsworth Publishing Company, 1986), 145–46.

    While often used interchangeably, as Professor Daniel Lagace-Roy notes, "Ethics is different than the term 'moral' … the distinction between ethics and morals is manifest in their particular aim: *morals* applies to the rules of conduct, customs, or beliefs by which people live and *ethics* is the study of the meaning of those rules, customs, or beliefs." Daniel Lagace-Roy, "Ethics," in Bernd Horn and Robert W. Walker, eds., *The Military Leadership Handbook* (Toronto: CDA Press/Dundurn, 2008), 262.

    Titus *et al.* elaborate on this idea, explaining that both ethics and morality mean "the custom or way of life." Modern usage of morality refers to conduct itself and ethics to the study of moral conduct. We speak of "a moral act" and "an ethical code." Titus *et al.*, *Living Issues in Philosophy*, 145–46.

    The *Dictionary of Philosophy* suggests that the term morality "is sometimes used as equivalent to 'ethics.' More frequently it is used to designate the codes, conduct, and customs of individuals or of groups, as when one speaks of the morals of a person or of a people." Dagobert D. Runes, ed., *Dictionary of Philosophy*

(Savage: Adams Quality Paperbacks, 1983), 218. For the purpose of this chapter, ethics and morals will be used somewhat interchangeably with recognition of the aforementioned definitions.

4. Brooks Peterson, *Cultural Intelligence: A Guide to Working with People from Other Cultures* (Yarmouth, ME: Intercultural Press, 2004), 214.

5. *Oxford Dictionary of Philosophy* cited in Lagace-Roy, "Ethics," 261.

6. *Dictionary of Philosophy*, *www.ditext.com/runes/e.html*.

7. Dictionary.com, *dictionary.reference.com/browse/dilemma*. Notably, dilemma is often used to define a situation where one has to choose between two equally desirable or undesirable options. See *Ethics in the Canadian Forces: Making Tough Choices* (Kingston, ON: CDA Press, 2006), 12. However, in its pure form the definition refers strictly to equally undesirable options. According to the *Philosopher's Dictionary*, "Correct use [of the term dilemma] refers to that sort of problem in which one has a choice between two unpleasant alternatives (called 'horns of the dilemma'). A moral dilemma is a forced choice between two incompatible but apparently binding obligations, or between two morally unacceptable alternatives — for example, when telling the truth would hurt someone, but lying would also be wrong." Robert M. Martin, *The Philosopher's Dictionary* (Peterborough, ON: Broadview Press, 1991), 65–66. As such, it might be a touch choice, but not a dilemma, to give one friend one million dollars and not another. It could be a dilemma, however, if you are forced to kill one of two friends and need to decide which one should live and which one should die.

8. It should be noted that *Ethics in the Canadian Forces: Making Tough Choices* defines ethical dilemmas in a different way. This text allows for dilemmas to be a choice between two equally desirable or undesirable alternatives. It then classifies three types of ethical dilemmas: the uncertainty dilemma, the competing values dilemma, and the harm dilemma. The uncertainty dilemma is defined as "a problematic situation where 'the right thing to do' is not clear." The competing values dilemma is described as

"a situation in which different ethical values support competing course of action." Finally, the harm dilemma is identified as "a situation in which any possible solution will cause harm or injury to others." A fourth category is identified as a personal dilemma where "in certain circumstances, dilemmas are deemed 'personal' because the course of action (right or wrong) is clear, but personal values (e.g., self-justice, friendship), or self-interest in the situation, contribute to the difficulty of acting." *Ethics in the Canadian Forces: Making Tough Choices*, 12–13. Although some differences exist, the definitions and explanations used in this text are meant to simplify and complement those found in *Ethics in the Canadian Forces: Making Tough Choices*.

9. This utilitarian approach to ethics, in which "the ends justify the means" — where the consequences of an act promotes the greatest happiness for the greatest number of people — originates with theorist John Stuart Mills. Notably, other philosophers have different views of ethics. For example, Aristotle believed that a virtuous person would simply know what the right course of action was. Immanuel Kant argued that the ethical status of an act does not rely on consequence. Rather, "An act has an ethical worth in accordance with absolute obligations." Lagace-Roy, "Ethics," 266.

10. *Ibid.*, 267–69. Also see *Ethics in the Canadian Forces: Making Tough Choices*.

11. Italics added by author.

12. *Ethics in the Canadian Forces: Making Tough Choices*, 15.

13. *Ibid.*, 16.

14. *Ibid.*

15. *Ibid.*, 17.

16. *Ethics in the Canadian Forces: Making Tough Choices* provides an excellent assortment of case studies for practising and discussing solutions to potential ethical dilemmas.

17. Peterson, *Cultural Intelligence: A Guide to Working with People from Other Cultures*, 213.

18. Department of Defense, *U.S. Army Counterinsurgency Handbook* (U.S. Skyhorse Publishing, 2007), 7–5.

19. Major-General Robert Scales, presentation at "Cognitive Dominance Workshop," West Point, 11 July 2006. It has recently been reported that "the Taliban is mounting a public-relations campaign to try to win the hearts and minds of Afghans with their own version of a field manual that urges efforts to limit civilian casualties. The little book with a blue cover, *Rules for Mujahedeen*, directs Taliban militants on how to behave while on deployment and how to deal with enemy combatants, treat prisoners of war and interact with civilians." Claude Salhani, "Taliban Field Manual: A Kinder, Gentler Militant?" *Washington Times*, 30 July 2009, *www.washingtontimes.com/news/2009/jul/30/ a-kinder-gentler-taliban*.

20. Beginning in 2004, accounts of physical, psychological, and sexual abuse of prisoners held in the Abu Ghraib prison in Iraq came to public attention. Notably, some U.S. military personnel were held accountable for the abuse. Subsequently, prisoners were sent to Iraqi led detention centres. As Sunni lawmaker Salim Abdullah noted of the abuse there, "The cases are as bad as what took place at Abu Ghraib, but it is painful when these things take place in Iraqi prisons. We met some of those who were released and saw the scars on their skins. They use different kinds of torture like tying the shoulders and hanging the body, which normally leads to dislocation of the shoulders." Deb Riechmann and Bushra Juhi "Allegations of Abuse in Iraqi Jails Raised as U.S. Transfers Detainees into Iraqi Custody," *www. newser.com/article/d99gie1o1/allegations-of-abuse-in-iraqi-jails-raised-as-us-transfers-detainees-into-iraqi-custody.html*.

Similarly, in 2007 Afghan detainees were reported to have been beaten following their release from Canadian to Afghan authorities. The publicity of each "scandal" eroded public support for the war efforts and events like these can be used by the opposition to erode support for their opponents. As D. Jonathan White noted, "Given the very public and regrettable failure on this issue [human rights] at the Abu Ghraib detention facility in 2004, the record of the United States has not been perfect in this regard either." D. Jonathan White, "Legitimacy and Surrogate Warfare," in Richard D. Newton, Travis L. Homiak, Kelly H. Smith, Isaac J. Peltier, and D. Jonathan White, *Contemporary Security Challenges: Irregular Warfare and Indirect Approaches*, JSOU Report 09-3, February 2009 (Hurlburt Field, FL: JSOU Press, 2009), 89.

21. David McKiernan, "COMSAF Counterinsurgency Guidance," *The Enduring Ledger Combined Security Transition Command-Afghanistan*, April 2009, 9.

22. *Duty with Honour: the Profession of Arms in Canada* cited in *Leadership in the Canadian Forces: Conceptual Foundations* (Kingston, ON: CDA Press, 2005), 23.

23. *Cultural Generic Information Requirements Handbook* (C-GIRH), DoD-GIRH-2634-001-08, 35.

Selected Bibliography

Cultural Intelligence

Altman Klein, Helen, and Gilbert Kuperman. "Through an Arab Cultural Lens," *Military Review*, May–June 2008, 100–104.

Bore, Henri. "Complex Operations in Africa: Operational Culture Training in the French Military," *Military Review*, March–April 2009, 65–71.

Coles, John P. "Incorporating Cultural Intelligence into Joint Doctrine," *IO Sphere: Joint* Information Operation Center, Spring (2006), 7–13.

Connable, Ben. "All Our Eggs in a Broken Basket: How the Human Terrain System is Undermining Sustainable Military Cultural Competence," *Military Review*, March/April 2009, 57–64.

Cultural Generic Information Requirements Handbook (C-GIRH), DoD-GIRH-2634-001-08.

Delp, Benjamin T. "Ethnographic Intelligence (ETHNINT) and Cultural Intelligence (CULINT): Employing Under-utilized Strategic Intelligence Gathering Disciplines for More Effective Diplomatic and Military Planning," *IIIA Technical Paper 08-02*, April 2008.

Earley, P. Christopher, and Elaine Mosakowski. "Cultural Intelligence," *Harvard Business Review*, October 2004.

Earley, P. Christopher, and Soon Ang. *Cultural Intelligence: Individual Interactions Across Cultures*. Stanford, CA: Stanford University Press, 2003.

English, Allan D. *Understanding Military Culture: A Canadian Perspective*. Kingston, ON: McGill-Queen's University Press, 2004.

Fontenot, Gregory. "Seeing Red: Creating a Red-Team Capability for the Blue Force," *Military Review*, September–October 2005.

Hernandez, Prisco R. "Developing Cultural Understanding in Stability Operations: A Three Step Approach," *Field Artillery*, January–February (2007), 5–10.

Ignatieff, Michael. *The Warrior's Honour: Ethnic War and the Modern Conscience*. Toronto: Penguin, 1999.

Kipp, Jacob, Lester Grau, Karl Prinslow, and Don Smith. "The Human Terrain System: A CORDS for the 21st Century," *Military Review*, September–October 2006.

Lynn, John A. *Battle: A History of Combat and Culture*. Boulder, CO: Westview Press, 2003.

McFate, Montgomery. "Does Military Culture Matter? The Military Utility of Understanding Adversary Culture," *Joint Force Quarterly*, 38, 2005, 45–48.

Ng, Kok-Yee, and P. Christopher Earley. "Culture + Intelligence: Old Constructs, New Frontiers," *Group and Organizational Management* 1 (2006), 4–19.

Peterson, Brooks. *Cultural Intelligence: A Guide to Working with People from Other Cultures*. Yarmouth, ME: Intercultural Press, 2004.

Puertas, Lorenzo. "Corporal Jones and the Moment of Truth," *Proceedings*, November 2004.

Salmoni, Barak A. "Advances in Predeployment Culture Training: The U.S. Marine Corps Approach," *Military Review*, November–December (2006), 79–88.

Simons, Anna. "Making Enemies: An Anthropology of Islamist Terror, Part I," *The American Interests*, Summer 2006, 6–18.

———. "Making Enemies, Part Two," *The American Interests*, Autumn 2006, 35–45.

Smith, George W. "Avoiding a Napoleonic Ulcer: Bridging the Gap of Cultural Intelligence," *A Common Perspective*, May 2006, Vol 14, No. 1.

Spencer, Emily, and Tony Balasevicius. "Crucible of Success: Cultural Intelligence and the Modern Battlespace," *Canadian Military Journal*, Vol. 9, no. 3, 2009.

Tamas, Andy. *Warriors and Nation Builders: Development and the Military in Afghanistan.* Kingston, ON: CDA Press, 2008.

Security Environment

Arquilla, John, and David Ronfeldt. *In Athena's Camp: Preparing for Conflict in the Information Age.* Santa Monica, CA: RAND, 1997.

Barnett, Roger W. *Asymmetrical Warfare: Today's Challenge to U.S. Military Power.* Washington, D.C.: Brassey's Inc, 2003.

Canada. *Counter-Insurgency Operations B-GL-323-004/FP-003.* Ottawa: DND, 2008.

Canada. "The Future Security Environment 2007–2030" (Draft). Ottawa, ON: DND, 2007.

Cetron, M.J., and Owen Davies. "55 Trends Now Shaping the Future of Terrorism," *The Proteus Trends Series*, Vol 1, Issue 2, February 2008.

Department of Defence. *National Defence Strategy.* Washington, D.C.: U.S. DoD, June 2008.

Didsbury, Howard F. Ed. *21st Century Opportunities and Challenges: An Age of Destruction or an Age of Transformation.* Bethesda, MD: World Future Society, 2003.

Friedman, George and Meredith. *The Future of War.* New York: St. Martin's Griffin, 1998.

Horn, Bernd, and Peter Gizewski, eds. *Towards the Brave New World: Canada's Army in the 21st Century.* Kingston, ON: DND, 2004.

Ignatieff, Michael. *Virtual War: Kosovo and Beyond.* Toronto: Viking, 2000.

Liang, Qiao, and Wang Xiangsui. *Unrestricted Warfare: China's Master Plan to Destroy America.* Beijing: PLA Literature and Arts Publishing House, 1999.

Neill, Don. "The Graduate Level of War: Continuity and Change in U.S. Counter-Insurgency Strategy," Defence Research and Development Canada Technical Report, 2008.

McConnell, J. M. "Annual Threat Assessment of the Director of National Intelligence for the Senate Select Committee on Intelligence," 5 February 2008.

Scales, Major-General (retired), Robert H. *Yellow Smoke: The Future of Land Warfare for America's Military*. New York: Rowman & Littlefield Publishers, Inc., 2003.

Schilling, William R., ed. *Nontraditional Warfare: Twenty-First-Century Threats and Responses*. Washington, D.C.: Brassey's Inc., 2002.

Schmidtchen, David. *The Rise of the Strategic Private: Technology, Control and Change in a Network Enabled Military*. Duntroon, AU: Australian Land Warfare Studies Centre, 2006.

Sloan, Elinor C. *The Revolution in Military Affairs*. Montreal: McGill Queens Press, 2002.

Smith, Edward A. *Complexity, Networking, and Effects-Based Approaches to Operations*. Washington, D.C.: CCRP, 2006.

Special Operations Forces

Adams, Thomas K. *U.S. Special Operations Forces in Action: The Challenge of Unconventional Warfare*. London: Frank Cass Publishers, 1998.

Arquilla, John, ed. *From Troy to Entebbe: Special Operations in Ancient and Modern Times*. Boston: University Press of America, 1996.

Barnett, Frank, B.H. Tovar, and Richard H. Shultz, eds. *Special Operations in U.S. Strategy*. Washington, D.C.: National Defence University Press, 1984.

Beckwith, Colonel C.A. *Delta Force*. New York: Dell Publishing Co., 1985.

Carney, Colonel John T., and Benjamin F. Schemmer. *No Room for Error: The Covert Operations of America's Special Tactics Units from Iran to Afghanistan*. Novato, CA: Presidio Press, 2002.

Clancy, Tom. *Special Forces: A Guided Tour of U.S. Army Special Forces*. New York: Berkley Books, 2001.

Clancy, Tom, with General Carl Stiner (retired). *Shadow Warriors: Inside the Special Forces*. New York: G.P. Putnam and Sons, 2002.

Cohen, Eliot A. *Commandos and Politicians: Elite Military Units in Modern Democracies*. Cambridge, MA: Center for International Affairs, Harvard University, 1978.

Dunnigan, James F. *The Perfect Soldier: Special Operations, Commandos, and the Future of U.S. Warfare*. New York: Citadel Press, 2003.

Gray, Colin S. *Explorations in Strategy*. London: Greenwood Press, 1996.

Harclerode, Peter. *Secret Soldiers: Special Forces in the War Against Terrorism*. Westport, CT: Greenwood Press, 1996.

Horn, Bernd. "Love 'Em or Hate 'Em: Learning to Live with Elites," *Canadian Military Journal*, Vol 8, No. 4, Winter 2007–2008, 32–43.

———. "Force of Choice: The Evolution of Special Operations Force Capability," *The Canadian Army Journal*, Vol 7, No. 3, Fall/Winter 2004, 99–110.

———. "When Cultures Collide: The Conventional Military/SOF Chasm," *Canadian Military Journal*, Vol 5, No. 3, Autumn 2004, 3–16.

Horn, Bernd, and Tony Balasevicius, eds. *Casting Light on the Shadows: Canadian Perspectives on Special Operations Forces*. Toronto: Dundurn 2007.

Horn, Bernd, David Last, and Paul Taillon, eds. *Force of Choice: Perspectives on Special Operations*. Montreal: McGill-Queen's Press, 2004.

Joint Special Operations University (JSOU). *Special Operations Forces Reference Manual, 2nd Edition*. Hurlburt Field, FL: JSOU Press, 2008.

Last, David, and Bernd Horn, eds. *Choice of Force: Special Operations for Canada*. Montreal: McGill-Queen's, 2005.

Lloyd, Mark. *Special Forces: The Changing Face of Warfare*. New York: Arms and Armour Press, 1995.

McRaven, William H. *Spec Ops: Case Studies in Special Operations Warfare: Theory and Practice*. Novato, CA: Presidio Press, 1995.

Moore, Robin. *The Hunt for Bin Laden: Task Force Dagger*. New York: Ballantine Books, 2002.

NATO. *AJP-3.5 Allied Joint Doctrine for Special Operations*. Brussels: NATO Standardization Agency, 27 January 2009.

Paddock, Alfred H. *U.S. Army Special Warfare: Its Origins: Psychological and Unconventional Warfare*, 1941–1952. Washington, D.C.: National Defence University Press, 1982.

Robinson, Linda. *Masters of Chaos: The Secret History of the Special Forces*. New York: PublicAffairs, 2004.

Smith, Michael. *Killer Elite: The Inside Story of America's Most Secret Special Operations Teams*. London: Cassell, 2006.

Spulak, Robert G. *A Theory of Special Operations: The Origin, Qualities and Use of SOF*. Hurlburt Field, FL: JSOU Press, 2007.

Thompson, Julian. *The Imperial War Museum Book of War Behind Enemy Lines*. London: Sidgwick & Jackson, 1998.

Weale, Adrian. *Secret Warfare: Special Operations Forces from the Great Game to the SAS*. London: Coronet, 1997.

Index

By the Same Author

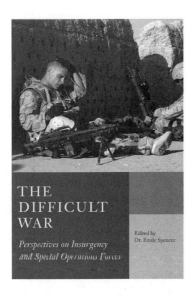

The Difficult War
Perspectives on Insurgency and
Special Operations Forces
by Dr. Emily Spencer
978-1-55488-441-4
$39.95

The Difficult War: Perspectives on Insurgency and Special Operations Forces is a collection of essays that deals with theoretical concepts related to insurgency as well as to the practice of irregular warfare. Since special operations forces are such an integral element to counter-insurgency, this volume also contains a large SOF component. Importantly, this book will assist the practitioner of the profession of arms to understand insurgency or, perhaps more accurately, counter-insurgency and those components that are germane to its practice. Moreover, *The Difficult War* provides insight and knowledge about these complex forms of warfare that are useful and accessible to both the lay reader and the military expert. As such the book is a valuable volume for those connected to or interested in the profession of arms.

Of Related Interest

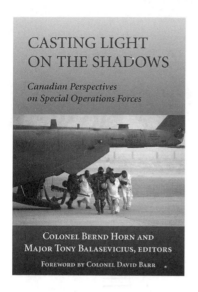

Casting Light on the Shadows
Canadian Perspectives on
Special Operations Forces
edited by Colonel Bernd Horn
and Major Tony Balasevicius
978-1-55002-694-8
$39.95

Special Operations Forces (SOF) have never been an integral element of Canada's military capability. Although units have existed periodically throughout the country's history, they have always been in the shadows. However, the terrorist attack in the United States on September 11, 2001, changed that. In the aftermath of 9/11, SOF became the force of choice. *Casting Light on the Shadows* consists of a series of essays on SOF-related issues written by individuals with specialized knowledge and expertise in the field. As well as providing a solid foundation for SOF theory, historical background, and evolution, the book also highlights ongoing developments in SOF.

Available at your favourite bookseller.

DUNDURN PRESS
w w w . d u n d u r n . c o m

What did you think of this book?
Visit *www.dundurn.com* for reviews, videos, updates, and more!